CHRISTMAS LETTERS

CHRISTMAS LETTERS

GARY ZACNY

Copyright © 2020 Gary Zacny
All rights reserved.

ISBN: 978-0-578-72005-0

For Ellen

Table of Contents

Foreword ....

Christmas Ornaments 1

Lovely as a Tree 6

The Christmas Star 12

Saving Christmas 18

Christmas Decorations 32

Bubble Lights 37

Carpe Christmas 42

Christmas Cookies 46

Ox and Ass Before Him Bow 53

A Perfect Toy 60

Hairy Christmas 66

Christmas Politics 79

Rio Christmas 85

Yule Haiku 95

Have Yourself a Merry Quantum Christmas 97

Snow Blue 103

Wintertime 110

Craft Hall Christmas 112

Advent 122

Home for Christmas 128

Christmas Tournament 134

Bonfire 150

Foreword

My habit over these last many years has been to write to friends and family a Christmas letter, a combination of holiday greetings, personal peeves, old jokes, new insights, and rambling reflections on toys, snowfalls, ornaments, and such trappings of the season. This book is a collection of such motley correspondence. It's a book about Christmas but not a book about religion – although I suppose something of religion seeps into everything human, since we anthropomorphize the universe. This book offers a humanitarian take on Christmas, because for many of us the holiday is less about sacrament than about tradition and the ways we create, at least once a year, a season of social comforts and affection and merriment.

Letter writing in this age of emails, texts and telecommunication may seem like a quaint enterprise. A letter is a throwback, a form of communication that has been familiar for thousands of years. The act itself, scratching a pen across a scrap of paper and sending it by carrier to distant readers, would have been familiar to a correspondent from the Roman Empire or the Ming Dynasty. The contents we might scrawl today are not so different from what Caesar or Marco Polo had to say. How's the weather? What are your kids up to? Where can I find a decent white wine?

Although letter writing is slow and old-fashioned, a leisurely pace may be a virtue. Letters encourage the writer to take a moment to clarify ideas, to re-phrase if necessary, to forego the spontaneity of conversation for the coherence of long thoughts. Reading letters is the complement, and letters offer more than sound bites, more meat than a tweet. Letters provide an excuse to relax, kick back and retreat from the bustling world to savor old stories, old jokes and old friends. Christmas letters, for me, offer quiet delights, small news and a nest of memories, a time for making and cherishing connections.

Whatever your traditions, your circumstances, your whims, I hope these letters will enliven your winter holidays and in some small way deliver the message of Christmas: Peace on Earth, Good Will to All.

Gary

Christmas Ornaments

[Upon compiling this stack of once-a-year writings into a book, I have discovered that the letters beg for some sort of organization. An anecdote from the 1980's, slammed next to a poem from the 1990's, followed by a story from the 2000's form – intentionally or not, produce a vague chronological sequence, am unintentional autobiography. This letter comes from media res, *the middle of things, my middle age in middle America.]*

Dear family and friends,

Many of us this time of year will lift a cardboard box from a dusty back shelf and set it gingerly on the dining room table. We will open it to find nestled there, each wrapped in paper towels or odd socks, a shiny hodgepodge of Christmas tree ornaments. That box, I think, is a perfect emblem of the season, filled with doo-dads fragile and foolish, useless and precious, things trivial as tinsel and yet riveting as a whisper from God.

Here's a handful of my favorite ornaments. That tiny brass trumpet comes from a holiday in New Orleans, and that wooden boy on a wooden sled was a gift from a childhood friend passing through town one December. That exquisite glass globe with the glass bead tassel comes from a trip to Florence, and the hand-painted angel fish is from Saint Lucia. There's a silver disc stamped like a helicopter commemorating a flight over the Grand Canyon, and that one, the homely carved wooden rod vaguely resembling a miniature totem pole, I bought that in Vancouver B.C. from a Native American artisan with hands like bear claws.

Look at the loopy smile on that ceramic bear with the fishing pole, a souvenir of a Colorado trout expedition. That one, the porcelain Snoopy wearing Santa's hat, comes from a caroling party held at our neighbor's home in the suburbs. We went ice skating on a frozen pond early one evening and then retreated to their fireplace to drink mulled wine and eat sugar cookies and all talk at once. Over there, that Santa wearing earmuffs came from a close-out sale at Marshall Field, and the icicle next to it from a rummage sale at church to raise money for the kid with leukemia. Those little crossed wooden skis on a string, they came from the ski trip to Steamboat Springs. My daughter twisted an ankle snowshoeing, and my son banged a knee learning to snowboard, and so the last day at the resort the two youngsters sat glumly by the fire and watched from the big picture window as Dad came schussing down the mountain. Later I searched the gift shop for a suitable souvenir of our week on the slopes. I had to settle for just the crossed skis. Too bad, though, a combination of one ski and one crutch would have been perfect.

Squished on the bottom of the box lies a wad of construction paper that resembles a lumpy cherry doughnut. It comes from a Christmas party long ago when we entertained guests by setting a table with red and green construction paper and doilies and ribbons and glue and sparkly stuff for people to make tree ornaments. A friend who is a physician and Jewish claimed that he had no experience with Christmas stuff, so he made an ornament to represent cirrhosis of the liver. A fine sentiment, really, the Cirrhosis of Christmas.

And now we are flying through space and time, back down the years. That fuzzy snow-white bear ornament comes from my Mother's retirement years, when she sat before the picture window watching the silent drift of snow and happily handcrafting soft cloth and bright yarn into teddy bears and candy canes and other gentle things. And that one too – yes, it's bedraggled now, but it was a stuffed gingham camel made by my daughter the Girl Scout, and if you lean close you might still catch a whiff of experiments with vanilla perfume or the scent of cherry cough drops stashed in her Brownie jacket.

Those silver-flecked ornaments are relics from another time. Grandmother passed them down to mother who passed them down to us. Shaped like spires, castle crenellations and Magi crowns, they must be seventy to ninety years old by now, hand-made blown-glass, manufactured before plastic molding became the norm, before childproof paint, before Underwriters Lab testing and government inspections and the homogenized bureaucracy of modern manufacturing. The glass is thin and fragile as a butterfly wing. These were baubles, trifles, not meant to last and yet they have survived being hauled out of a box and hung on a tree, year after year, for multiple lifetimes. Sometimes sentiment is a better preservative than concrete walls.

Wedged in a corner of the box lies a great treasure wrapped in Kleenex. It may look like an ordinary red glass ornament stamped with the words "Silent Night", but the thing radiates memory. It comes from an old-fashioned ornament set we hung when I was six years old, the year my second cousin George came to spend the Christmas holiday. We were told that George had only recently come to America and that during the war he was in a Nazi concentration camp. My parents treated George tenderly, like a fragile glass ornament.

We liked him instantly despite, or maybe because of, his funny accent, his intense quietness and his gaunt figure, pale as a ghost. He drank in the American Christmas. He kept smiling and smiling. His eyes filled with wonder when he spied the table laden with fudge and cashews and platters of cookies. This for a boy who lived for years on nothing but potato soup. And he laughed aloud to see the gleaming snowmen embroidered on Aunt Velma's sweater -- this for a boy who wore rags and slept under a lice-infested blanket. I was too young to know what his story meant, but I remember that somewhere toward the end of the evening, when the house was filled with hooting and hollering and colorful shreds of torn wrapping paper, George grew still more quiet. He retreated to a place terribly, terribly far away.

Dickens had it right. We can fly through time and space on a whim. On a cold winter night, sitting hunched before a flickering fire, all alone in robe and slippers, we are never really alone. We can raise the lid of a battered cardboard box to behold a hundred ghosts fly out, whispering, giggling, bobbing against the ceiling like a hundred colored balloons.

May your Christmas spirits be benevolent,

Gary

Lovely as a Tree

[Here's an early Christmas letter, written in the 80's or 90's when my children were still small and I thought nothing of acting as chauffeur, lumberjack, construction foreman and home decorator – all before breakfast!]

Dear Friends and Family,

Last year I broke down and bought an artificial Christmas tree. For decades I got real trees – fir and scotch pine and balsam. I liked the smell, but of course that lasted only a day or two. And then there was the whole rigmarole of bumbling through a slushy tree stand in a converted parking lot, and paying an alarming price for a dubious hank of pine and jamming it in the car and hauling it home and sawing the bottom somewhat straight and erecting the thing and stringing up recalcitrant bulbs and daily watering the dying plant and sweeping up debris and finally dismantling the corpse and hauling it to the recycling center with nothing to show for it but needles in the carpet.

So I bought a plastic tree and it was perfect. It sprang from the carton clean and glossy and a rich forest green. It went up without muss or fuss. It came with its own stand, and assembly was a breeze. The branches attached to the aluminum trunk in concentric circles, and as they snapped in, I bent the giant pipe cleaners into branch-like shapes. The assembled object was tall, dark and handsome. It had a pleasing shape, the very prototype of a spire. It stood in the morning sunlight, splendidly erect, stately, photogenic.

And yet, and yet, and yet. Something was missing. It wasn't just the fragrance – although I admit that I love the smell of fresh-sawn pine. It wasn't the simple, pleasant puttering of lopping off ungainly branches or pinching the trunk in a tree stand. It wasn't the small thrill of seeing the creature arise – although I admit that every time the tree went up my heart wanted to shout "Thar she blows!"

It was missing, I think, something like a sense of wildness. A real tree might have bald spots and scars and twists in the trunk, and I liked that random element. A real tree might shed a few needles the way an old dog might shed a little fur and give you the good karma of acceptable nuisance. A real tree might come with a tiny bird's nest tucked among the branches, or a stranded pine cone or a bit of string tied to a deflated balloon. A real tree had a history.

When I was a kid the family tradition was to accompany my Dad to the Kroger Grocery parking lot to pick out a tree. We yammered and haggled and generally selected a passable fir. The tree may have been lop-sided and scraggly in the parking lot, but at home and arrayed with lights and ornaments and tinsel, it became a scullery maid transformed into a princess. It was lovely, or at least modestly lovely, like Cinderella's squinting, buck-toothed sister.

When I became the Dad and charged with bringing in a tree, I decided we should have something special for the kids. For the sake of tradition and authenticity, we should cut down our own tree. We lived in the northwest suburbs of Chicago at the time, and an hour's drive north brought us into rural country dotted with fields/stands/copses/groves of evergreen. My two pre-teen kids voted to pull into a tree farm at the edge of Round Lake Beach with rows of tall Scotch pine and a warming house at the back of the field. The kids hopped from the car and ran ahead so that they could hide just below a rise. A few minutes later, when Dad appeared at the top of the hill, encumbered with a map and handsaw, they sprang up with an Apache war cry and descended on him flinging a hail of snowballs. After Dad was good and pelted, the war party retired to the warming house for steaming mugs of cocoa.

One year we drove to a nearby garden center and tree nursery which was going out of business. A victim of suburban sprawl, the nursery was torn up preparatory to building a housing subdivision. A clump of magnolias lay uprooted at the edge of a gravel drive, and bulldozer tracks had smashed a yew hedge. Here and there stumps among the evergreens testified to a brisk business.

A man at the edge of the lot said, "Twenty dollars and you can cut any tree you find." The children whooped and swarmed among the trees, eventually selecting a magnificent 30-foot tall spruce with thick blue-green branches at the top. I thought, well okay, lumberjack it is, and I felled the huge tree. We sawed off the bottom ten feet and still had a hard time strapping it to the van and hauling it home.

We had suburban sprawl of our own at the time, a rambling California-style home with a cathedral ceiling. The twenty-foot high splendor of spruce fit the living room just fine. We hauled out a step ladder and decked it with twinkle lights and garlands. Neighbors, friends and visitors oohed and aahed at the magnificent tree. Everyone agreed that it was the biggest and best tree ever.

And yet, and yet, and yet. I never passed that tree without a twinge of guilt. It was too much. It was woefully out of place in a suburban living room. It was like dragging a fallen monarch into the room and dressing him in gaudy clothes to amuse the crowd. It was King Kong in chains.

Decking the halls with boughs of holly dates back to at least Roman times, when indoor garlands were part of Saturnalia. The Germanic pagans brought trees indoors, perhaps as an act of worship -- or at least, knock on wood, for good luck. It's a tradition that immigrants brought to

America, a quaint custom that caught on, and although it began harmlessly enough, it has become big lame-brained business.

Times have changed. A tree is no longer part of Nature's boundless bounty. Everything green and growing on this planet is under threat. They have soured the oceans; they are burning off the Amazon jungle; they have depleted the Ogallala Aquifer; they have polluted the Gulf of Mexico; they have plowed under the prairie and now they're paving the parks. I don't fully understand the economics of it – and maybe a reusable plastic tree consumes more resources than a dozen years of whacking live ones – but I resist the idea of killing a living thing for a silly reason.

And maybe now I'm being silly, and a tree made from recycled soap bottles is no more eco-friendly than a real tree harvested from a farm. But it feels the opposite of silly; it feels adult. People must develop an aesthetic of stewardship for the planet that extends to koala bears and dung beetles and the blue spruce. We inherited this blue-green planet and we ought to pass it along to our children and our children's children. So, for me this year, it's time to do my part and put up an artificial tree.

Only, maybe a day or two after the Christmas bedlam, I'll make time to get outdoors, perhaps an afternoon of cross-country skiing or a tramp in the woods. I'll pause beneath an evergreen and take a deep breath of fresh pine scent and just stand there a few minutes, feeling the quiet strength of the trees, the meditative stillness, the beauty of green boughs beneath an immaculate blue sky.

Plastic Christmas trees have a place in the scheme of things, but they will never entirely supplant the thrill of wildness dragged home in a fresh-cut tree. Perhaps we need a bit of both, the slick modern version and the rough-hewn original. Myself, I find comfort in the company of trees. They stand like sentinels between us and the blight of the merely man-made, embodying the rightness of the natural world.

Happy holidays, and hugs from a tree lover,

Gary

The Christmas Star

[How does one sign off a Christmas card or letter? Before I compiled this book, I would have said that I just sign my name. Maybe add a formulaic M.C. and a H.N.Y. But on review I discover, no, I usually feel compelled to add a little something. A personal note (see you in Peoria) or a wider appeal (regards to your car pool) or a blessing (may your stockings and your olives be stuffed). Maybe it's an unconscious impulse to delay departure, like touching fingers as the jetway doors close.]

Dear friends and far-flung family,

Last Christmas we planned a wow moment for our two-year-old grandson, Liam. We cut a shapely, stately Douglas fir at a local tree farm, hauled it home and mounted it in the living room. We strung lights, hung ornaments, draped old-fashioned crinkly tinsel on the branches and topped the whole shebang with a gold foil star. That evening we coaxed Liam into the living room, flipped a switch, and behold -- a shining resplendent Christmas tree in gauzy glory! Liam laughed and gurgled and raced to the foot of the tree. He pointed to the high tiptop of the tree and said, "Flower!"

It's no wonder the star caught Liam's eye. It always catches mine. There's something about a star atop a Christmas tree, or beaming from a Christmas card, that evokes the spirit of Christmas. It's quiet as pawprints in snow; it's gentle as candles in the window; it seems an emblem of something far, far away and greater than ourselves, and yet near and tender and beaming down at us like a lover.

The Star of Bethlehem was not a big part of the early Christian narrative. It's just a throwaway detail. In fact, the Gospel of Matthew in the New Testament is the only place this "star" is mentioned in the Bible (Matthew 2:2, 7-10, King James Version). Even there, information on the star is more suggestive than descriptive. The key phrasing is Matthew 2:9:

When they had heard the king, they departed; and, lo, the star, which they saw in the east, went before them, till it came and stood over where the young child was.

Science struggles to make sense of the ancient text, and scientific explanations abound: maybe it was a comet, a meteor, a nova or supernova, or perhaps a conjunction of planets like Jupiter aligned with Mars – because people in Biblical times referred to planets as "wandering stars". But science scratches its head and frowns because all such explanations have problems. No known comet was in the night sky anytime around the probable birth date of Jesus, and meteors and ball-lightning and such phenomena embellish the night sky, but their light does not last, and no trail of a nova has been detected, and the planets were not aligned, and even if they were, in no sense would they stand in the sky or direct the caravan of Three Wise Men. Perhaps a flying saucer or UFO could do so, but let's not get into that.

For the faithful, scientific explanations do not pertain. Who cares, really? The Christmas star was a marvel nested in a miracle packed in a singularity, and it delights humanity to believe we are special and that a newborn child is really special, and that, my friends, is all we need to know.

Science tells us that light travels at 300,000 meters per second. This means that, in a single year, light travels one light-year (duh), and that means that the light of the Christmas star is just about to reach a planet 2000 light-years hence.

I like to think about that distant planet, and how sentient beings that resemble giant stalks of broccoli are just now waking up to a new and wondrous blur in the sky. I like to think of green alien teenagers sitting on a front porch swing, hand-in-hand-in-hand, spooning beneath the light of their three moons, and how they might gasp in wonder at that sudden flash in the panoply.

If you want to understand how integral the star is to the Christmas story, you need only attend the annual Christmas pageant at your local church. You don't need to be a Christian to appreciate a Christmas pageant, any more than you need be Muslim to enjoy the call to prayers. It's just a beautiful moment.

Any Christmas pageant is a travesty – in the technical sense – and perhaps I should explain that term. A travesty (and bear with me, you non-bookish folks), the *genre* known as "travesty" in literary studies is defined as the opposite of the "mock-heroic". The mock-heroic gives us a grandiose, epic-like treatment of a trivial subject. Alexander Pope's "Rape of the Lock" is a classic example of the mock-heroic, since it narrates a trivial event (someone snipping a lock of hair), and tells the story in the highfalutin language of Homer's Iliad. Travesty is the contrary form, a serious or sacred event treated with frivolity. The works of Gilbert and Sullivan present the solemn proceedings of the courtroom or the royal navy as a string of silly satirical songs, a travesty. A Christmas pageant dramatizing the events surrounding the birth of Jesus, surely a holy story from Christian tradition, presented by children costumed as sheep and angels and bearded wise men, presents us with, in the nicest sense, travesty.

My second favorite character in the Christmas pageant is the Star of Bethlehem – my favorite, of course, being the doddering camel that accompanies the Three Wise Men. The star shining over the stable (or the Christmas creche) lends an element I cannot do without. Starlight is a must. It casts soft, glimmering light on the scene, giving everything gravity and an aura of tenderness like a halo. It makes even cardboard scenery look majestic.

To understand the dramatic effect, you need to attend and absorb such a pageant:

When my kids were young, they appeared in a Christmas pageant at the local Pentecostal Church. We were not members there, or even regular church-goers, but our family was invited by well-meaning neighbors to participate in their happy drama. My ten-year-old daughter stood in the wings, dressed as a shepherd in a cut-down bathrobe, with a crook and a *keffiyeh* and tightly curled paper beard. My six-year-old son tried to get into the character of a sheep – or perhaps a goat, or even a donkey – the costume being a generic animal-face, more suggestive than realistic.

The nativity scene materializes slowly. The pastor recounts the story of Christmas, the taxes from Caesar, the rugged journey for a pregnant woman, the scarcity of lodging and the family bedding down in a stable. The drama accelerates, unfolding chaotically and joyously as eager children, wearing wire wings and haloes, cherubic, rosy-cheeked and oblivious to the proceedings, wander onto the stage. Oohs and aahs spring from the congregation as a baby is born and an angel toots a horn and a heavenly host (enacted by the congregation) sings praises. Now shepherds appear (cue my daughter) followed by their flocks (cue my son) and a schmear more angels arrive, and the tension builds. At last a star appears, Ta-dah! the most flamboyant showoff from the youth choir, resplendent in gleaming gold. Immediately the star is followed by a trio of kings with rhinestone crowns and bristling dyed beards and then camels and then more angels and then cows and goats and then still more angels and everyone is singing and the mother Mary is beaming she is so happy and everyone is so happy.

May the peace of this quiet season be with you, may the good will of this merry season be with you, may the star of Christmas lighten your heart,

Gary

Saving Christmas

[What I wanted to say about Christmas this particular year took the form of a story, or a couple of stories. And why not? When we gather over the holidays with friends and family, that's part of the fun, the chance to share old times, and new times, the chance to hear and tell stories. It seems to me a jolly, humane way to spend holidays.]

Dear family and friends,

Part I

Christmas is the season when we disregard the avalanche long enough to regard the snowflake.

We forget sometimes in the crush of holiday busyness – the shopping and baking and traveling and whatall – what a fragile thing is true Christmas. Fragile as a snowflake. Christmas for most of us descends like a spirit, intangible, transient, sometimes small and easily lost. Sometimes it needs saving.

I was about six-years-old one particular Christmas and crazy with longing. I had asked Santa Claus for a special gift, a genuine air-powered Roy Rogers ping pong ball shooting rifle. My pal Francis Hildeberg got one for his birthday, and he used it to shoot clothespins off his mother's laundry line. Once he whopped his big brother in the back of the head with a ping pong ball and became for a few days our neighborhood gang's icon of glory.

All my longing came to a focal point on Christmas Eve. My parents were soft-hearted people who couldn't stand to see their kids frustrated at holidays, and so they allowed the children to open presents a little early each Christmas Eve. Every year we gathered around the Christmas tree, my parents and all four of us kids, and assorted aunts and uncles, and even a few neighborhood friends who joined us for punch and carols and the intoxicating atmosphere of anticipation.

The day of Christmas Eve passed as slowly as a freight train hauled by ox and asses. We went about our business, baking gingerbread or stoking the old coal furnace, but from time to time we walked past the Christmas tree. Beneath the tree packages wrapped in bright print paper and tied with silver ribbon gleamed in the shadows. By the time dinner was finished and the dishes cleared, the living room was strewn with people and playthings. In one corner Aunt Velma sat in a rocking chair, knitting and chain smoking. Lazy spirals of smoke rose to the ceiling forming Aunt Velma's personal cloud. At her feet lay an abandoned Monopoly game and beside that a plate of oatmeal cookies for Santa already half eaten. Uncle Joe, in brown corduroy trousers, took up half the sofa, all thighs and elbows, absorbed in a crossword puzzle. My little sister

Lynn kneeled on a chair at the dining room table, making ornament angels from paper doilies and library paste. My oldest brother Bob sprawled on the rug, trying to figure out how to use a cribbage board. My other brother Jim sat cross-legged beside Grandma and showed her card tricks.

"Grandma, pick a card, any card," he said. "No, not that one."

Mom walked in from the kitchen drying her hands on a dish towel. She shooed us kids down to the basement. Our family custom on Christmas Eves was for the kids to wait in the basement, playing darts or cowboys-and-indians among mason jars and bric-a-brac, while the adults remained upstairs nipping a little eggnog. After a half hour that seemed like a month, we kids would hear a jingle of sleigh bells signaling the arrival of Santa Claus. We would rush up the stairs, always just barely missing the departure of old Saint Nick, to behold the living room transformed. Garlands decked the dining room table, multi-colored lights flashed in the living room window, streamers hung from doorknobs and the living room floor was crowded with big new packages: a bicycle with a chrome headlight for Jim, a sleeping bag and canteen for Bob, a pink plastic miniature oven for Lynn complete with a light bulb for baking cupcakes, and for me a long thin package wrapped in green paper.

With a collective whoop we kids descended on the gifts. Lynn ripped open a package to reveal a doll in pink pajamas. When she tilted the box horizontally the doll's eyes closed like a baby sleeping. She didn't even remove the doll from its box before she tore open another package to reveal a vial of bubble bath. Bob held up a baseball glove shouting "Hey, it's a Stan Musial!" Jim bounced a wad of Silly-Putty against the wall. Aunt Velma removed a set of linen handkerchiefs from a small box and inspected the monogram. "Oh, they're lovely. Thank you," she said to the surrounding hubbub. Then she went back to her cigarette.

The living room floor grew thick with torn wrapping paper and bedraggled ribbon. It looked like it had been hit by Santa's reindeer at full gallop. Dad emerged from the kitchen at this point carrying a cardboard box. "Here," he growled, "don't make a mess. Put your paper in the box and save your bows in this plastic bag." We kids looked at each other for a moment. We knew that Dad delivered the same speech every Christmas just as the gift orgy was approaching its climax. Instantly, gleefully, we ignored him and tore into more gifts.

My heart pounding, I slipped ribbon and paper from my "Santa gift" to behold – my heart's desire! A genuine air-powered Roy Rogers ping pong ball shooting rifle! It was a yard-long beauty, a gleaming aluminum tube, the barrel, nestled in a brown plastic genuine artificial wood grain stock and below the barrel a hand pump and behind the pump a trigger guard. At the bottom of the package I found three ping pong balls.

Inserting a ball in the plastic seal ring at the end of the barrel, I pumped the rifle vigorously. I could hear the plastic parts tense and feel air pressure gripping the barrel with the promise of power. Like Roy Rogers facing cattle rustlers in black hats I smiled grimly, serene but stern, and took aim at a glass angel dangling from the Christmas tree.

With a loud pop! the rifle went off. I didn't actually pull the trigger. I'm sure I didn't touch the trigger. The ping pong ball flew across the room and smashed the glass ornament to smithereens.

Shouts, shrieks, conversation in the living room all collapsed like a carousel going down a garbage disposal. My little sister whimpered. A few scraps of wrapping paper fluttered to the floor. The whole family realized as one that the Forces of Darkness had entered our home. Mother's cherished angel ornament was gone and she was fighting back tears. Father soon would stalk into the room bristling with anger to administer curses and perhaps a spanking. Christmas was ruined.

Just at that moment Dad did walk into the room. He had been in the kitchen, perhaps doctoring the eggnog, when he was attracted by the silence.

"What's going on?" he said. No one answered. He regarded the ping pong ball at the base of the Christmas tree, and he squinted at the glass fragments, and he turned to me, holding the genuine air-powered Roy Rogers ping pong ball shooting rifle.

"Let me see that," he said. He took the rifle in his big hands and turned it this way and that. He stooped and picked up another ping pong ball. He pushed the ball snugly into the barrel end and worked the pump action. He frowned at the little rifle, and then in one swift motion he whirled, brought the rifle to his shoulder, and fired at the Christmas tree. Pop! The ping pong ball shot across the room and hit a red ball dangling from a high branch. The ball exploded into flecks of red and silver. We sat up in stunned silence, jaws agog and eyes blinking with astonishment.

Dad flinched like a man caught sneaking the last slice of mincemeat pie. "Well, I'll be jiggered!" he said, "I never really thought it would work."

We all burst out laughing. Christmas was saved! Mother was laughing, Dad was blushing and laughing. Uncle Joe nearly choked on a macaroon, he was laughing so hard. Lynn danced in merriment and then dropped to her knees and began clawing at the wrapping paper for more presents.

And me, I laid aside the genuine air-powered Roy Rogers ping pong ball shooting rifle and whispered an anonymous prayer of relief. Lost amid the flurry of wrapping paper and the tinkle of happy voices, my heart grew light as a snowflake and I had my first taste of salvation.

Part II

Ten years later to the day I found myself in the high school gymnasium on Christmas Eve morning. I had joined a teen group called Jive Alive, which held sock hops in the gymnasium and taffy-pulls in church basements and thereby kept the adolescents free from a life of crime. Jive Alive was a stupid name invented by our parents to show that they were groovy. We teenagers accepted the name the way we accepted most things, gracelessly and without question.

It was a good club though. We built floats in the annual Founders Day parade; we painted shop windows in the small downtown business district with goblins and witches each Halloween; we hosted an annual fish fry to raise money for a bus trip to Chicago to see the buildings and meet kids from other small towns.

This particular Christmas Eve was another annual event: Holiday Basket Giving. The teen group took some of the money left over from dance admission fees and the teen building Coke machine. We bought big wicker baskets and filled them with Christmas goodies – canned hams and tangerines and raisins and teddy bears and mittens. Each basket was crammed to the brim and tied with a big gold ribbon.

We met at the high school gym where the adult sponsors passed out names and addresses of the recipients. I had my Dad's car, so I packed half a dozen baskets into the trunk and took off with my friend Danny Macarthy to play Sons of Santa Claus. We took baskets to the poor section of town on the other side of the oil refinery, an area known as Little It-lee. It was fun, and I got a kick out of the big eyes of the little children when they spotted us at the door. One woman in a housecoat seized the basket and peeled a tangerine and began eating before we left. At another home we were met in the doorway by a man in a sleeveless t-shirt. Our adviser had told us that many of the men in this neighborhood were on strike from the steel mill, and they had been out of work almost six months. "Whaddya want?" the man had barked. We explained that we were from Jive Alive and we had brought a Holiday Basket, and we held out the gift. He took the basket while a small child standing at his legs tried on tiptoe to peer into the basket. The man produced a weary smile then and he called after us, Thanks! and we answered back, Merry Christmas!

Holiday Basket Giving was going great as we took our last basket to a dilapidated frame house just behind the lumber yard. The porch was three steps of poured concrete, cracked and stained with mold. The sagging gutters were choked with leaves. The gravel driveway held a black oil stain the size of a bath tub. Through the picture window I saw a crowd of small children, one in diapers, playing on the floor of a dimly lit room while a small television on the back wall blinked in the darkness.

I rang the doorbell, but it didn't seem to work, so I knocked. After several knocks the door swung open to reveal a teenaged boy wearing jeans and a torn sweatshirt with a baby perched on his hip. Even in the faint light I recognized a classmate from school, Malcolm Murray.

"Malcolm –" I said, and then I ran out of things to say.

Malcolm regarded me with sheer amazement. I had never visited his home before, never met his family, never even seen him on a weekend. He was one of those kids known from horsing around in the cafeteria or trading spit wads during study hall. He was never in my college prep classes, and he worked after school so he never went out for sports. Just a skinny kid in floppy clothes who greeted everything – homework and fickle girls and smelly locker rooms – with the same loopy smile.

He started that loopy smile as he shifted the baby from hip to shoulder, and then he spotted the Holiday Basket. He swallowed hard and his eyes filled with angry tears.

"No," he said. "We don't need that. Go away."

"Aw look. We only want– C'mon, Malcolm."

He shut the door in our faces. We knocked again, but there was no answer, and after a few minutes on the concrete porch feeling foolish, Danny and I went back to the car and drove back

26

to the teen center. We got another name and delivered the Holiday Basket to another part of town and that was that. We were young, and easily distracted. No doubt that Christmas evening we went on to a party or movie or a family gathering and never gave another thought to Malcolm Murray's mortification.

But that incident soured my faint friendship with Malcolm Murray. We were never best buddies – just study hall buddies. We used to play a game on the way home from school. I would usually miss the last bus because I was delayed at football practice or basketball practice, and I would be dragging my weary bones up Whitelaw Hill toward home. Malcolm would be leaving his job at Krasky's Doughnut Shop and he would appear on his battered Schwinn bicycle at the top of Moeller Hill. By mutual unspoken consent our coincidence on the hills constituted a race. I sprinted downhill as fast as I could go. Malcolm pedaled for his life, legs pumping and books flying. We zoomed to the bottom of the hills and skidded to a stop in the vacant flower shop parking lot. Panting and wheezing we leaned against the brick wall and, no matter who won, we debated the race results.

"Get a horse, [gasp] you hopeless duffer."

"I beat you [gasp] by a mile [hiccup], you hopeless gas bag."

"Aw, [groan] you couldn't beat a turtle on crutches."

"Yeah, [groan] you couldn't beat a snail struck in quicksand."

We would survey the evening sky from the empty flower shop parking lot. Maybe Malcolm would share a bag of stale doughnuts, and maybe I would share peanut butter sandwiches leftover from lunch. And the first stars would appear in the evening sky like luminous moths. When we left the parking lot for our cold suppers, we were filled with a nameless peace.

All that changed after the Holiday Baskets. We never raced again. Malcolm was shy with me in the hallways, and he never dropped by my table at lunch. We hardly spoke another word for the remaining two years of high school, and after graduation I lost track of him.

Malcolm's story doesn't end there entirely, however, because, fast-forward five years and I was home from college and lounging around my parents' house the morning of Christmas Eve. I was bored out of my skull. I sat at the dining room table sipping coffee and smoking and scowling. I was kicking myself because I had passed up a chance to join some college buddies skiing. A friend had offered me a ride to his parents' summer home in Wisconsin, with assurance that his parents would not join us and that the weekend promised some serious drinking and maybe some girls. But I didn't feel like another round of boozing, and I couldn't ski, and I wanted something else. I didn't know what I wanted, but I thought I would spend time with my old folks, and hang around the old neighborhood, and maybe something would happen.

Nothing had happened. The old home town was pathetic, candy cane stripes on the lamp posts and cheap plastic garlands in shop windows. A rinky-dink *papier-mache creche* in the middle of main street, with lambs that looked like albino pigs and three Wise Men dressed in bathrobes. None of my friends was around. My days consisted of cornball carols on the radio and cigarettes and bleak gray skies. I wondered what I had been thinking, to pass up the ski trip, because Christmas offered nothing but commercial hype and silly television and stale memories. Christmas was for kids, and I wasn't a kid anymore.

The doorbell rang, and because Mom was busy in the kitchen baking nut bread, I answered it. On the porch a young man in a soldier's uniform stamped his feet against the cold. I blinked a couple times before I recognized Malcolm Murray. He looked great, very fit, taller than I remembered and ramrod straight in his olive uniform with shiny brass buttons. He was holding something behind his back.

"Malcolm, son of a gun. Come on in."

"Sorry," he said. "I can't. I only have a 24-hour pass and I need to go see my family. But I wanted to see you."

He looked down at his gleaming boots, and then he looked up to catch my eyes. His gaze was very clear, very steady.

"That time back in school, you remember, with the Christmas basket, I got it wrong. I mean I took it wrong, and I've thought about it a lot. It's been bothering me. You were only trying to do us a kindness, I understand that now. And I got all huffy and spoiled it. And we shouldn't despise kindness, you know? And I wanted to say I'm sorry, that's all. Just – Merry Christmas – and I'm sorry"

"Aw jeez, man, sure. It's okay."

Malcolm thrust at me a green wine bottle tied with red ribbon. "I brought you something," he said, "for you and your family."

I took the bottle. Cold Duck, domestic sparkling burgundy, straight from the grocery store and tied with red ribbon. "Well thanks. This is unexpected. I don't have anything for you. "

"That's okay," he said. "That's the point."

"Are you sure you can't come in a minute? My Mom would love to see you. Maybe a cup of coffee?"

"No, really. Gotta see my folks. I just wanted to see you before I ship out for Germany. Just to wish you a Merry Christmas. Merry Christmas, you hopeless gas bag."

Malcolm strode down the porch steps and swung onto the sidewalk. His walk had changed.

30

He moved with strength and purpose, not a march exactly, but more erect and bouncier than I remembered. A few scattered snowflakes fell from the empty sky like the last leaves of autumn. Malcolm's figure dwindled, and then he turned the corner and was gone.

I returned to the kitchen bearing the bottle of Cold Duck like it was the Holy Grail. Such a small thing, really, a kindness on a gray winter day. My mother looked up from a pan of steaming nut bread. A layer of snow had accumulated in the corners of the kitchen window, like a ribbon of crystal. Mother noticed some change in me because she wondered aloud who was at the door and what was wrong. I told her nothing was wrong, but I couldn't explain the essence of it because I couldn't explain it to myself. My smile was so wide you could have hung ornaments in the corners of my mouth and used me for a Christmas tree.

I couldn't explain to her that an old friend had stopped by to save Christmas.

Happy holidays, and a taste of salvation,

Gary

Christmas Decorations

[*Don't ask which Christmas this is. 2003? 2004? After a few decades, the Christmas holidays begin to glom together like shards of peanut brittle left out in the sun.*]

Dear Friends and Family,

This Christmas I am overwhelmed by things. Things to buy and things to see and things to do and things, things, things. And it's partly my own blamed fault. After decades of kicking around the world a person can accumulate a lot of things. And the collection expands when you get married and combine your wife's things and your own. Take, for instance, Christmas decorations.

When I descend the basement stairs and survey in one corner Ellen's stacks of Christmas boxes and in another corner my own heap, I get smacked between the eyes by the 2x4 of Christmas. Ellen has candles and ornaments and lights galore. Tree ornaments, of course, but also tree skirts and tree stands and tree garlands, and probably hidden in there somewhere a tiny elven tree surgeon. Myself, I have boxes of holiday stuff, a rather tasteful collection of keepsake ornaments but also a former popcorn garland that looks like a giant necklace of spitballs. There's an old string of lights as big as Japanese lanterns. Scrunched in a corner lies a silver bell that fell off a rent-a-horse in Grant Park and a somewhat-used Santa Claus candle that resembles Burl Ives in drag. We have boxes and boxes of Christmas stuff, enough to sink a ship. No kidding, you could load our Christmas *fol-de-rol* on the stern of the Titanic, stand back, and watch her tilt nose up and slide to the bottom of the sea.

A part of me, the right brain which is relatively sane, thinks this is too much. My idea of house decorating for the holidays was best summed up by one of Ellen's friends' daughters. The kid had come home from college with a roommate to share Christmas break. Both girls were as worldly and cynical as only sophomores can be. When the daughter walked into her parents' home and caught a glimpse of hallways festooned with snowmen and elves, she backed out of the place, slammed shut the door and turned to her girlfriend with a stricken look. "OMG!" she said, "Christmas has puked on our house!"

My idea of a good house decoration hearkens back to when I was a sophomore in college (true story). It was Homecoming weekend, and the University of Illinois at Urbana was awash in crepe paper and banners and cornball school spirit. The air trembled with the old school song, and the freshmen were wearing blue and orange t-shirts – or was it blue-and-orange beanies? The fraternity boys and sorority girls had hung blue and orange balloons from the rafters; the Alpha Sigma Something house had built an enormous Trojan Horse out of crepe paper and adorned it with a huge banner that said "BEAT WISCONSIN!"

I was a GDI (God Damned Independent) and far too worldly and cynical to participate in the frivolities of Homecoming Weekend. It was pathetic how old geezers (the 40-somethings) visited the campus to re-live their undergraduate shenanigans. I felt no envy for the false gaiety and the hullabaloo of Homecoming. Well, maybe a little envy. In youth, most of us walk a fine line between independence and loneliness.

I was walking home from the library that night, my coat collar turned up against the chill October air, pretty much ignoring the crepe paper dangling from dormitory windows and the heavy metal music blaring from open doorways. Something tiny caught my eye, a faint glowing on the front porch of a small boarding house. I walked closer. It was an empty peanut butter jar and inside it a single small candle flickering. I walked still closer. Inside the jar, behind the small candle, lay a strip of cardboard with something written on it. I leaned still closer. Hand-lettered on the strip of cardboard, it said, "Homecoming . . . yay!"

And that's the way I feel about Christmas decorations now. All the gaudy lights blazing from the bushes, the inflatable snowman warbling from the azalea bed, the life-size sleigh and eight bright-lit reindeer on the roof – it's all too much. We get carried away. A simple birthday party for a fellow who celebrated Hanukah, and we have to turn it into a big production with loudspeakers blaring and strobe lights flashing and garlands sparkling. Inside the house it gets even crazier – wreaths on the refrigerator and snowman soaps in the bath and hand towels embroidered with carol lyrics. The television channels are flooded with carolers and snowmen and bangled trees and gingerbread men. The magazines sport recipes for fruit cake, Santa cookies, gooseberry pie and cranberry punch. The commercials beckon to us, sing to us, scream at us, stun us and waylay us. I begin to fear I've OD'ed on Christmas.

Some folks, of course, like a bit of holiday cheer in the form of twinkling lights and angel statues. Sure, I understand that. By and large it's harmless fun – not to mention big business – and with the coming of the winter solstice we all need to make a statement, something like a declaration shouted in the face of vast descending darkness, something that says, "I am here, by golly, red and green and right out loud I declare I will get through this winter and greet the spring."

Sure, I understand that. But a thing is what it is in relation to other things. A star might be a thermonuclear engine to an astrophysicist, but it might equally be a signpost to a shepherd boy. The holidays might be better if they were not jammed among things gaudy and crass and loud. Maybe we would all be better off if we deflated the snowman bobbing above the yew bushes. Maybe we should forget about the mango-pineapple-pomegranate punch and just sip a nice cup of tea. Maybe we should pull down the reindeer on the roof and the phalanx of elves at the gate, maybe we should re-think the guest towels embroidered with Chris Moose and we should silence the satellite radio booming "Twelve Count 'Em Twelve Days of Christmas." Often the silence is an improvement.

That's what I recommend, if only for a few minutes. Bundle up, walk outside and stand in the chill night air for a minute or two. Put away the Godiva chocolates and taste a snowflake on the tip of your tongue. Let the cold night sink in, and feel how it must feel for those who are cold and hungry and outcast on such a night. Let your thoughts flow to the connectedness of things, how your life beautifully and improbably has been touched by a child born in a stable two thousand years ago. Hear the silence. Douse the Christmas lights and see the stars.

A peanut butter jar with a candle is a small thing, but it can be a wonderful thing, if it illuminates an ageless wish for Peace on Earth Good Will toward Men.

Happy Hanukah, Happy Kwanzaa, Christmas … yay!

Gary

Bubble Lights

[*It's hard to place the year of this letter, 1980's perhaps or early 90's, when I was a young man with young children, seeing them lit up like rosy-cheeked angels by the glow of tree lights.*]

Dear friends, and what the heck, enemies too, after all it's Christmas,

Hanging tinsel is no job for amateurs. It takes a certain flair, a certain panache, a certain élan, aplomb or *savoir faire*, a certain *je ne sait qua*. Perhaps the French have a word for it. It takes a delicate touch and a discerning eye to hang tinsel properly on a Christmas tree.

When I was a kid, we decked the Yule tree with glass ornaments and garlands and slivers of thin metal foil – genuine tinsel, not the idiot-proof Mylar stuff they use nowadays. Tinsel was my specialty because I was terrible at stringing together popcorn puffs with needle and thread to make a garland, having five thumbs per hand, and I was terrible at hanging little candy canes on the branches because an alarming number disappeared in the process. Therefore, I took special pride in hanging the tinsel.

Oh sure, it was possible to bestow tinsel carelessly. My kid sister would hang strips of tinsel for a few minutes and then grow bored and fling a handful at the tree, leaving tangled clumps splashed willy-nilly on the lower branches like wisps of metallic Spanish moss. No doubt she was in a hurry to rush outside and eat the lemon snow. But I was an *artiste*. I would stand back from the tree, inspecting it for places where the scraggly branches left gaps in the imagination. When I spotted a bare branch, I would drape gracefully a filament of tinsel just so. Adroitly placed, the tinsel produced an icicle effect that would fill the bare spot with a silvery shimmer.

Our tree those many years ago wore a hodge-podge collection of old-fashioned cone-shaped electric lights, like glowing gum drops on a string. We had one or two leftover light bulbs shaped like angels or hummingbirds. My favorite kind of tree light was a sealed glass tube set atop a plastic lotus-shaped housing. When the tiny light bulb heated the water in the sealed tube, it began to bubble. All night long it would glow red or orange or green and bubble merrily. I could sit and watch endlessly the column of swirling bubbles.

Later I got interested in the physics of the thing. The heat of the bulb agitated the water or alcohol in the tube, obviously, and the liquid gave off a dissolved gas, probably air, and the air formed spheres in the liquid and being buoyant rose up the liquid column and burst into the air pocket at the top. Then it struck the glass at the top of the tube and cooled and dissolved again into the liquid and convection currents carried it to the base of the light where it grew hot again and started the cycle all over. I found it fascinating that such a simple, tiny rigmarole in a tube could be so beautiful.

When my children were still in booty pajamas, I bought our household a string of bubble-lights, now somewhat updated with smaller bulbs and thinner plastic housing. My kids would study the busy bubbling tubes with mixed curiosity and delight. Watching them watch the rising bubbles made me think of my own childish delight – and that's a great thing about kids, how they bring back the openness and wonder of your own childhood – and then I got to thinking about how my own parents must have watched me bemused by bubbles, and maybe that made Mom and Dad recall the simple pleasures of their childhood Christmas decorations, and maybe they too felt a rush of fondness for their parents, my Grandpa and Grandma, and how the grown-ups made an extra effort to give the children things bright and upright and merry on Christmas Day.

That recursion of tenderness forms one of the unspoken joys of Christmas. Today's kindness evokes yesterday's kindness and all the tides of kindness past. That's why we cherish traditions surrounding Christmas. We need tradition like we need air. The impulse to preserve a bunch of tree ornaments in wads of Kleenex, the need to bake a batch of gingerbread men just like old Aunt Rhoda, the ceremony of erecting the Christmas tree in the parlor, sprinkling a bowl of eggnog with just a pinch of nutmeg – these are all homage to tradition and things larger than ourselves. Grandmother delighted Mother who delighted me so that I would be eager to delight my daughter and she would want to delight her daughter, and on and on, through the generations, ripples of love.

There is something moving and expansive for me in that idea. Spiritual experience is that which lifts us out of ourselves, makes us think of larger things, like the whole sweep of generation after generation propagating harmless amusements, and the universality of those feelings, how a kid in China or Peru or Alabama will look with delight and wonder upon ascending, gurgling bubbles.

Christmas time makes me muse on things spiritual. At my Unitarian church, I get static for such talk -- because most of the congregation are materialists – some downright dialectical and some just plain crass. They pooh-pooh the whole idea of the Spiritual, the anthropomorphic Christian God, because they say it's all just a lark of the imagination, and not real, not testable or scientific or worthy of a second thought.

And maybe they are right. And maybe they are wrong.

Perhaps we got it all backward. We say that rocks are solid and rock walls are reality and spirits are nothing but illusions. That's why we think ghosts can walk through walls, because they are nothing more than insubstantial illusions. But perhaps it is we who are insubstantial and transient as passing thoughts. Spirits may be so real, so dense that they can walk through walls and trees and our bodies as easily as we walk through shadows. Perhaps it is we who are the illusion.

What is real and what is not flits through my mind and pops into nothingness like rising bubbles. I think that bubble lights are beautiful, and that beauty is real enough. Bubbles may be nothing more than burps in the ether, just shapes made by microscopic forces of adhesion and convection and such. But I feel they are real enough, and they rise and shine gloriously, if only momentarily. And feelings have meaning.

At this time of peace and goodwill, I hope that the spiritual and the material will peacefully co-exist. Those who celebrate God become human should join in joyful chorus with those who celebrate the longing for godliness that is human.

May your Christmas Spirit bubble merrily,

Gary

Carpe Christmas

[This letter has a definite time stamp, the year 2013. It was a momentous year, but then, aren't they all?]

Dear friends, family, flora, fauna, folks and all the ships at sea,

    This year more than usual I have been thinking about history, the history of America and my own little patch of it. The year 2013 is the sesquicentennial of the Emancipation Proclamation. It's the 150th anniversary of the year when Yankees and Confederates fought the Battle of Gettysburg. Ellen and I visited the national cemetery at Gettysburg in October. We stood where Lincoln spoke words that still ring in the air. We rode horseback over the battlefield and encountered among the corn fields a small grove of trees where Pickett's men hid while awaiting orders for their gallant, doomed charge up Cemetery Ridge. We grew solemn, straining to hear over the creak of saddles ancient ghosts whispering along the bridal path that wound through that quiet strand of blood orange maples.
    Also fifty years ago marks a more personal event, the occasion of my high school graduation. Ellen and I drove six hours south to my old home town for the reunion. It tickled me to see those

wrinkled, stout, gray-haired geezers with their grinning buoyant adolescent faces shining through. People were gentle and gracious at the reunion party. I likened them to "good eggs" because all the hard edges and gnarls of youth had been knocked off by the bumps of life, leaving them universally smooth, well-rounded, good eggs.

The year 1963, I realize with mild shock, was also the year President Kennedy was assassinated. My sister Lynn and I took an Amtrak train this November all the way to Dallas to visit brother Bob and his family. Not a word about the assassination was spoken during our 24-hour ride to Dallas, not a word was mentioned at my jolly high school reunion, and then suddenly in Dallas the news was flooded with remembrances and images from the Kennedy years. I had forgotten how handsome he was, and how elegant his wife, and how painful those days as we sat before our black-and-white televisions and watched the pomp of a state funeral. I remember the riderless horse trailing the coffin. Some events in life strip away all frivolity and show us as the bare, forked creatures we are.

And my excursions to the past took me to the even more remote past. Ancient America popped up during two Sierra Club service trips – one to Catalina Island off southern California where I ran into a Hollywood project leftover, a herd of buffalo that wandered through our campsite at night – and another at Pyramid Lake,

43

Nevada, where our group of campers worked alongside the local Paiute tribe helping them stock the lake with cutthroat trout. Also this summer, I toured another Native American site, the famous Cahokia Mounds and museum near my old home town. At the museum I peered at dioramas showing how the First People hunted and gathered buried their dead before their civilization went belly up. Humanity seems ephemeral as summer grasses, from the vantage point of anthropological displays that purport to capture 500 years of history in a few glass cases. Peoples come and peoples go, nations rise, cities climb to the sky, and it all drifts away without much trace. The Mound builders, Lincoln's noble cause, American Camelot, all shimmer in the heat of the moment and then vanish like a mirage.

Well, this is supposed to be my Christmas letter. And what does all that have to do with Christmas? It means, perhaps, that we should savor the passing moment because it all passes so quickly. I have reached an age when ten Christmases can pass before my eyes like an old newsreel. I see a beloved aunt, now long buried, arriving in a puff of snow with a twinkle in her eye and a Merry Christmas on her lips. I see kids gathered around the ping-pong table downstairs awaiting the arrival of Old Saint Nick and the hullabaloo of gift-giving. I see a Christmas turkey, big as a buffalo, steaming and golden, lifted onto the dining room table and Dad with glittering knife and fork about to carve the bird for the family jammed around the table like a wolf pack around the latest kill.

I see ten Christmases roll by, or a dozen or three score, and they all blend together into a whirlwind of sugar cookies and wrapping paper and snow shovels and squeals of laughter. And I think how it all passes away so quickly and so completely. And how we ought to keep it somehow, keep it in our hearts for a dark drab day. Put away a little Christmas like a piece of wedding cake to be brought out in an emergency like a sky rocket of sweetness.

So that's my advice and my wish for you this Christmas. Don' let it wash over you and be lost in the swirl of the next day and the next. Seize this Christmas, *carpe* Christmas, and make it the best and brightest you can.

And I wish you a hundred more just as merry,

Gary

Christmas Cookies

[*This letter takes me back to the late 1990's and a hard year.*]

Dear family, friends, and cookie monsters (you know who you are),

It started perhaps twenty or twenty-five years ago, when I was just divorced and living with my teenage son in a shabby apartment in Mundelein, Illinois. The world was a dreary place in those days, with slapdash man-made dinners of beans-and-franks and Spaghetti-os, the usual temper tantrums at home, a long slog commute to work, and work a tedious grind, and yet the best thing I had going all day. Christmas rolled around and sharpened the pangs of weariness, disillusion and loneliness. What a load of crap is Christmas, I thought. Yet something in me had the strength to protest. I wanted it to be better for myself and my child, and so I thought, what the heck, it's Christmas, I'll bake some cookies.

To my faint amazement, the mere act of breaking out the baking pans made me perk up. Baking took my mind off things. I bought sacksful of baking goods – flour, butter, sugar and spice – I fired up the oven and rustled up some old recipes and tuned the kitchen radio to a station playing nothing but Christmas carols. Seized by the demon of confectioner's sugar, I brought out the neglected electric mixer, the disused measuring cups, some plastic ice cream containers for mixing bowls, and I began to bake.

I started with raisin oatmeal cookies, adding extra butter to keep them chewy and a half cup of molasses to give them sweet voodoo. The smell of baking began to lift my spirits. With a couple dozen oatmeal cookies under my belt, and a few burnt ones *way* under my belt, I turned to pecan sandies. You might call them Russian tea cakes, or Mexican wedding treats, but I like to think of them as Scottish pecan sandies, dry as a golfer's sand trap and sweet as a birdie in the morning. The trick with sandies is to chop the pecans fine, so they mix evenly in the rich buttery dough. Bake them until just brown on their fat bottoms, and then dust the results with powdered sugar, so that on the first bite the dry center elicits a burst of saliva which plasters sweet dust to the palate followed by a satisfying nut crunch and a flood of buttery satisfaction. Pecan sandies, okay, check.

Holly cookies are nothing more than the classic Rice Krispy treats, only made with corn flakes to give the cookies a gnarly texture like holly, and colored bright holly green. I spooned the sticky holly lumps onto waxed paper set on the kitchen table and topped them with cinnamon drops for holly berries. They glistened next to the cooling batches of oatmeal and pecan cookies.

I was bushed by the time I finished three kinds of cookie. I sat at the kitchen table, out of breath, and a thin film of sweat or condensed steam had formed on my forehead. Baking was a lot of work. I was about to call it a day when my son Nathan wandered into the kitchen, lured no doubt by the noise and the cinnamon aroma. He was a polite kid, a bit sulky like most teenagers but also more gentleman than I. He asked if he might sample the cooking. I nodded, yes, sure, and when he bit into the oatmeal cookie and I watched his eyes light up, I felt inspired. That was all I needed, and I lunged back to the oven.

Now I was getting the hang of it. I mixed eggs with lemon bar filling right out of the box, and I baked two pans of lemon bar crust, and while that was in the oven, I mixed peanut butter dough according to the recipe in Mom's <u>Better Homes & Gardens Cookbook</u>. I removed the crust from the oven and spread filling on top and shoved the pans back in the oven and set the timer to 25 minutes. While that was baking, I shaped the peanut butter dough into balls and rolled the balls in crystalline sugar and set each one neatly on a pan and squished them flat with a fork. I removed the double batch of lemon bars, set them on the window sill to cool, then inserted the peanut butter cookies into the still steaming oven.

While those baked, I made fudge from sugar, butter, chocolate chips and marshmallow paste. Sugar dissolved in butter and marshmallow melted into thickening liquid and melting dark chocolate chips swirled in the golden goo. Now I was rocking. While stirring the fudge sludge, I kept removing trays of peanut butter cookies and inserting more cookies and mixing cocoanut flakes with egg whites for fluffy macaroons, and pressing milk chocolate chips into the peanut butter rounds and slicing maraschino cherries to top the macaroons and give the batch a touch of Christmas red.

After several hours of baking, I flopped down on a kitchen chair, doused the radio blaring "I Saw Mommy Kissing Santa Claus," and surveyed the results: oatmeal and pecan and holly cookies, fudge and lemon bars and macaroons, and a couple dozen good old sugar cookies shaped like snowmen in white icing with jelly orange slices for carrot noses. I was completely tuckered, too pooped to brush the powdered sugar from my t-shirt, and I felt something funny. What was that? Oh, yeah. It was happiness. It felt like Christmas.

Now many years of baking have passed, and Cookies for Christmas has become a household tradition. Every Christmas season these last twenty years I have baked treats. My good wife Ellen has joined in with gusto. She added Florentines and berry crisp and walnut fudge wreathes (and thank the stars, she does half the work). We make hundreds each year, arranging them on waxed paper in tin boxes to give out to friends, neighbors, church buddies, postal carriers, newspaper delivery boys and anyone else who looks like they could use a sweet lift.

We feel good handing out cookies. A box of sweets may not be as fancy as gold, frankincense or myrrh, but it's the thought that counts. Maybe giving is not better than receiving, but it's two sides on the same coin.

People praise me, my family members are amused, the church ladies are astonished, old friends invite me in to have a cup of tea, to reminisce and mutually munch the goodies. Your family probably gave birth and nursed and raised to great heights a number of such holiday traditions. Something in human nature makes us stumble upon a good thing and then repeat it and enlarge it until it becomes an irreplaceable part of life's routine: tradition, the thing we would not do without. I find that baking is a fine way to get in the spirit of Christmas.

Think of it. Things as simple as flour, butter, sugar and heat, and we make of them myriad delights, a stream, a river of sweetness and light. Humanity may suffer from the Sins of Ice – avarice, cowardice, prejudice, and the pride that turns our hearts to ice. But we also find redemption in something wholly humble and homely. Cookies are proof that we have it in us to become angels.

Here's wishing you this season Happy Holidays, clement winter, the occasional brush with your heart's desire, and yes, and of course, cookies,

    Gary

Rose in Snow
[Dear family and friends, this year, a poem:]

I.
A rose in snow
Green and crimson swathed in white
Trembles in the bitter night
Born too late to grow.
In the village down below
Brights bedeck the tallest tree
Children shout with greedy glee
Skaters glide upon the ice
Shoppers ponder fad's device
Punch and laughter flow.

Then from the East a star shines forth
And from the West and South and North
Missile madness wrath is nigh
Fireballs blossom from on high
Planet glows in fiendish light
Beasts in stables shriek in fright
Hosts of cherubim take flight.
All hopes and fears expire tonight.

A flawless snow
Nothing grows where mushrooms grow.
The land an ashen waste of white
Nuclear winter, silent night.

II.
Let us speak now, you and me
As we gather 'round the Christmas tree
Of things which can but must not be.

Starting with the gift of fire,
Man proceeded to conspire,
Applying science to the task
Of turning humans into grass.
Swift invention power brings
To exterminate all living things.

Who can wield this awful might?
Whose the vision, whose the right?
Nations wrangle, people flail,
Rules, religion, reason fail.
War awaits, the stocks increase.
What can promise lasting peace?

Christmas gives us one small clue
For how to start the world anew.
Hope blots reason, faith trumps law,
Utterly simple as a bed of straw,
Peace will spring from our resolve
To build a world that's ruled by love.

We cannot know
That spring for us will ever thaw
The hate and hurt that mortals flaw,
But hope's slim tendril pushes so,
We yet may grow
A rose in snow.

Peace on Earth,

Gary

Ox and Ass Before Him Bow

[This letter went out some decades ago, then got lost in a box of abandoned Christmas cards, then resurrected and a bit touched up here. The issues and sentiments have not changed much in the intervening years, nor have we.]

Dear family, friends, fellow passengers,

It's Christmas season again, and I've just been out walking the neighborhood and ogling Christmas house decorations. Our neighborhood observes a mostly secular Christmas, heavy on the Santa Claus and snowmen, but light on angels and nativity scenes. A small creche, however, caught my eye. It stood in a sheltered corner by the garage, not large, lighted simply by a single small floodlight. Just a ceramic depiction of the star overhead, a porcelain Holy Family, three Arab kings on camels, shepherds and a smattering of barnyard animals – oxen, donkey, sheep and a dog. Someone's child had stuck a plastic toy dog at the end of the line of animals. I liked that innocent addition to the creche, a dog by the manger. It seemed to fit the scene.

There's a charming legend attached to the Christmas story that tells how the animals in the stable on Christmas Eve began to speak. The story is not part of the Biblical version, and it may be just an ancient folk tale glommed onto

Christmas, the way Santa and reindeer and other stories have been attached to the narrative over the years. But I like the way the miraculous comes alive around Christmas.

I try to imagine what the animals gathered around the feed trough might say. Surely the cattle are doing more than lowing. The oxen and asses, the goats and sheep too might make small talk, if they could for once have a say. The cow gazes down lovingly at the Christ child and says "I will give him milk to nourish his body" and the sheep says "I will give him wool to keep him warm" and the ass says "I will carry him to ease his burden" and the camel says "My feet hurt."

Perhaps the animals belong in a creche because we need to re-think our relationship with all creatures in light of the pervasive kindly spirit that comes with Christmas. We have not been kind to animals, and we ought to do better. We humans have gone from fearing the wolves at our door to stocking them in Yellowstone Park. We love animals and keep millions of animal pets, everything from dogs and cats to turtles and tarantulas. Yet we use and abuse animals – we trap them and cage them, we beat and flay and slay them. We steal their young, and for crying out loud, we eat them. Perhaps we need to pause a moment in this innocent season to consider our burden of collective guilt.

My daughter and son have become vegetarians – and my new son-in-law too. For the younger generation, foregoing meat seems to be more than a dietary fad. It seems to be part of a new consciousness, a realization that humans must become stewards of the earth and therefore obliged to preserve the animals, all animals, rather than exploit them.

Plenty of folks in these days are dead set against farming animals and slaughtering them for meat, fur, hides and tallow. Vegans even go so far as to resist animal exploitation of any kind. They refuse to consume eggs, they refuse to wear leather shoes, they won't drink the milk that ought to feed calves and kids. Some folks even refuse to consume fish products – although our mammalian prejudice seems to make fish consumption okay. Even conscientious vegetarians may occasionally snarf down a salmon fillet. There are no protesters marching outside canneries.

I don't know, I'm not sure, I doubt if I could give up hamburgers out of aesthetic or ethical qualms, but I am beginning to see the rightness of it. It's hard for old-timers like me to accept the idea that we have been wrong to breed and use animals all these centuries. Maybe I am growing old and maudlin, but I hope not so old that I cannot rethink the tenets of kindness. I am beginning to hear the squealing of the piglets and the silence of the lambs.

Society becomes unworkable if we afford animals the same compassion which we think we owe mankind. Just do the math. Seven million Jews were executed by the Nazis in the six years of WWII, and that makes us shudder. But in terms of killing, that is just a drop in the bucket of blood. We slaughter 39 million cattle each year to stuff our gaping maws. And another 23 million pigs and over 500 million sheep. Each year. More than 200 million animals are killed for food around the world every day – just on land. That comes out to 72 billion land animals killed for food around the world every year. Imagine the cemetery that could accommodate such carnage.

People say yes, but those beasts are not thinking creatures like us. No animal rises anywhere near the level of human intelligence. There's no campaign to Save the Worms. Yet we know that intelligence is a spectrum of abilities. Science is only now catching up to common observation, but new research in animal intelligence has discovered logical crows, bilingual apes, playful otters and singing dolphins. Science can now prove that animals are smarter than we ever imagined. If harpooning a lovesick whale is a crime, then what about bludgeoning a randy boar? If we butcher and eat 39 million steers per year, isn't it likely that one of those millions is a genius and more valuable, peaceful, and likeable than the asses that roam the halls of Congress?

Nobody cares about animals more than those who make a living from them. A farmer may pen up and later castrate and still later slaughter a bunch of hogs, but that same farmer gives more serious attention to his pigs' welfare than the city folks who gnaw its barbequed ribs. On my grandfather's farm we learned early that raising animals is an honorable vocation, hard and sometimes brutal work, but intimately tied to social good. Grandpa was a no-nonsense user of animals. He refused to feed the cats that hung around the farm house (except, when they were young and helpless, he might squirt milk from the Guernsey's udder into the mewling kittens' pink mouths). He said that cats had to earn their keep, same as you and me, and he wanted them kept a bit hungry so that they would be eager to catch the rats that ate the grain.

On the farm we kept a mixed-breed sheepdog, Old Shep, a mutt of many parts, part work animal and part pet. Grandpa let Old Shep sleep on the porch because he was useful. He scared away the foxes that stole chickens, and he kept watch at night. Despite his breed, Old Shep made a good hunting dog. He became expert at scaring up rabbits during the fall hunting season, until one November when Grandpa accidentally hit him with a load of buck shot. After that, whenever Grandpa or one of the men in the family took down a shotgun, Old Shep would disappear behind the barn and not be seen again for hours. Eventually, Old Shep became a family legend.

The story goes that Grandma spotted a large rattlesnake in the yard, and terrified that it might bite one of the children, she chased it with a fury, but it slithered back to its hole and disappeared under the farm house. Grandma told Shep, "Sic 'em" and the dog, ever obedient, crawled under the base boards of the house and attacked that rattler. There was a fierce battle of sorts, growling and banging against boards, and after a few minutes Old Shep emerged with a limp, very dead snake in his jaws. During the battle the snake had bitten Old Shep. After a few minutes his muzzle swelled up big as a football. Old Shep staggered to the horse trough and sank his muzzle in the cold well water. He lay there for three days, not moving or eating or even whimpering, just staring with woeful eyes at the sky, as the sun rose and set and rose and set on his pain. But after three days, the swelling went down, and Old Shep rose to his feet and limped back to his favorite rug on the farm house porch. Grandma loved him after that. She used to sneak him food scraps and even sometimes fresh meat when we had slaughtered a hog.

Eventually Old Shep grew feeble with age. His muzzle turned white, he went blind, and he limped around the house on his three good paws, but in obvious pain. Late one fall afternoon Grandpa carried old Shep deep into the woods. He carried Shep, and a shovel too, and wrapped in a burlap sack the 12-gauge shotgun. After a couple hours, long enough to dig a grave, Grandpa returned to the house. He said not a word, and we knew Grandpa would never cry, but his eyes grew soft when he glanced at the empty rug on the porch.

It's no wonder that animals creep into the Christmas story (and Easter and Thanksgiving too). They are part of all that humans have seen and sought and accomplished. We have shared the planet with them forever. We have welcomed them in our homes for ten thousand years. We have befriended them, worshipped them, anthropomorphized them, dehumanized and slaughtered them, but never understood them.

Next time you pass a Christmas creche, don't just glance at the Christ child, or admire the bejeweled kings of the East, but regard the animals too. Sculptors take pains to show that the animals are participating. They belong there, beside the manger, standing in straw, gazing down quietly at the baby. Dimly, and humbly, they seem to understand. They belong there and make it whole.

In this season, let us strive to make a place for our fellow passengers on the Ark that is Earth.

Peace on Earth, good will to all, even the lowliest among us,

Gary

A Perfect Toy

[*This letter was sent out somewhere around the turn of the millennium, but it comes from a time when I was very young, adventurous and primed for infatuation.*]

Dear family, friends, and especially the children,

There was a time when the most wonderful thing I could imagine was a ring, a Captain Midnight Secret Decoder Ring. It was a perfect object. The ring itself was made of brass, a pretty valuable metal, and the brass was ideal because it was so thin and flimsy that it could be bent to fit very small fingers. And mounted on that thin brass band was a cube-shaped plastic fitting that glowed in the dark, and ensconced in the plastic was a thin disc of burnished aluminum so shiny that it could be used to flash Morse Code messages to compatriots across an enemy valley. Most cunning of all, the plastic housing held a secret compartment, just the right size to hold a strip of paper bearing secret code. To access the hidden compartment required a technique of thumbing aside a panel covering the tiny, mysterious, glow-in-the-dark, possibly radioactive hidden compartment. No blood red ruby, mounted in gold, encrusted with diamonds, could compare to a Captain Midnight Secret Decoder Ring.

This amazing ring arrived via a mail-in offer printed on the lids of Ovaltine jars. My heart leapt when I received the package in the mail, the first item ever addressed to me alone. I tore open the wrapping to discover a small cardboard box, and opening the box found nestled in a wisp of foam the gleaming decoder ring. I put it on then and there, admiring the pea-green plastic setting, the gleam from the signal-flashing aluminum oval, the swash and the heft of it. In the secret compartment I inserted a message in code: "Irls-gay Are-yay Oopid-stay". I wore it for two or three days, I slept with it on my finger, I dreamed of carrying the ring through forest and desert and jungle, and then I lost it.

It still gives me a pang to recall the catastrophe of losing the ring. Where could I have dropped it? Perhaps on the playground, perhaps the swimming pool, perhaps in the vacant lot behind Gieselman's house where we played Indian Ball and rounders. It seems to me that all the remaining days of my life I have been searching for that ring – or if not the ring, then the joy of its possession. My precious.

As Christmas approaches, I have been searching for something like that ring, a perfect toy to present to the children in my life. I have foremost in mind the smallest one, the toddler grandchild, but come to think of it, I ought to consider toys for other grandchildren and my own grown kids and for children of friends and, sure, the friends themselves and you too, my friend. Because who among us doesn't enjoy a toy – as long as it's the right thing at the right time?

What would make a perfect toy? For my grandson when he was just one-year-old, the gift was irrelevant. He got more fun from the wrapping paper than the doo-dad inside. And while the two-year-old gurgled over some bright plastic gizmo, he was equally enthusiastic about the box in which it arrived. As he grows older, he may play with the thing, the toy, a few minutes, but quickly he will return to the group and the ceremony of gift-giving. What he will really want is just to be the center of attention, the center of the universe, a princeling basking in rightful homage of parents, family and all the subjects of his realm.

What is a toy, anyway? I guess anything could be a toy. A child makes wrapping paper a toy, a rubber band a toy, soap bubbles a toy. Any child will make food a toy – just watch the kid shove a forest of broccoli beneath a toy mountain of mashed potatoes. My first wife and I, trying like everyone else to be the best parents on Earth, determined to raise the new generation free of gender roles. We gave a Raggedy Ann doll to our son and a miniature John Deere tractor to our daughter. But it didn't matter. Gender seems to shine through. The girl picked up a stick, wrapped it in a cloth and made it a doll. The boy picked up a stick, pulled an imaginary trigger and made it a weapon. Toys reflect preoccupations of the mind.

What isn't a toy? Surely a hammer, a hoe, an ax – and yet we make "toy" versions even of serious adult things – toy trucks and toy airplanes, toy kitchens and operating rooms, even (alas) toy guns and toy soldiers. For small children, playing with toys is serious business, so maybe toys are not the things in themselves but rather the attitude we adopt toward them. They are springboards to play, blasting caps to explosions of imagination, rockets to unreachable stars. A toy is something you can take seriously for a moment and then abandon, like imaginary teacups filled with air tea.

Not just anything can be a toy because some things we are not to be abandoned. Maybe that is one of the great lessons of growing up. People are not to be toyed with. Corinthians tells us "When I was a child, I spake as a child, I understood as a child, I thought as a child: but when I became a man, I put away childish things." Toy not unto others, as you would have them not toy unto you.

A perfect toy ought to appeal to the character of the child receiving it. An affectionate child might play with a snuggly stuffed animal or a dolly with overlarge lifelike eyes. A curious child might want a curious contraption. That was me as a youngster – a budding nerd before we had a word for nerd – I'd gravitate toward "educational" toys. My delight was the microscope and kaleidoscope and periscope – because some of us like to scope things out. Most kids want a toy that's marvelous and yet actual, since they inhabit a space where the phrase "real magic" is no oxymoron.

And it's not just kids. Think of all the simple pleasures in life that arise from toys. In past times small tots got little toys, like whistles, jacks, jump ropes, pogo sticks, skateboards, Slinky, Silly Putty, and card games like Old Maid and Authors and Crazy Eights. Then, as ageing children, we got big toys – snowboards and season tickets and motorboats and Maseratis. Toys are things we discover and enthuse over and then discard all lifelong. If you think a sailboat is not a toy, then okay, maybe if you are hauling fish to market, the boat is not a toy. But if you are standing in the prow wearing a yachtsman's cap or imagining that you're Captain Blood in leather leggings, then yeah, a boat's a toy.

The perfect gift would, like the Captain Midnight Secret Decoder Ring, fire the child's imagination. It would launch some great adventure, point the path to one's destiny, provide a way to relish and comprehend and so to master the bristling, threatening, fascinating larger world.

This Christmas letter is my attempt to give you folks, young and old, near and far, something like a toy. We all resemble nested Russian dolls, bearing within us the secret life of a child, and within that a smaller child, and within that a child smaller still. What a fine gift it would be to resuscitate that inner child in a cynical pre-teen, a preoccupied young adult, a middle-aged divorcee, a crotchety old man, me and you.

Wishing you this season a moment, an hour, or a day when you find the perfect toy,

Gary

Hairy Christmas

[This letter was mailed a few years ago, when I stepped back to gain perspective on myself, as recent retirees are wont to do, to see the trajectory of my life and decide how best to spend the remaining years. Somehow that meditation and the usual Christmas greeting got all mixed up with hair.]

Dear family and friends, innocent bystanders, curious onlookers and idle passers-by,

About a year ago, on my 67th birthday, I retired from 40-odd years of work as a systems engineer, management consultant and computer roustabout. Since then I have been lurching about trying to find my sea legs and continue the voyage of life. I took an art class drawing charcoal portraits, cleared trails during two Sierra Club trips, volunteered for phone banks and door-to-door canvasing in the national election, played in two tennis leagues and caught up on lots and lots of reading. I have discovered the truth in what all my friends told me: when you retire you will become so busy that you'll marvel at how you ever found time to work.

Naturally, my sense of priorities has changed. When I was working, breakfast meant scanning the headlines as I gulped coffee and rushed out the door. Nowadays at breakfast I have time for two or three cups of coffee, and while I wait for the coffee to cool, I ponder the morning crossword.

One project I created for myself is growing hair. Not body hair, although with age the body continually surprises us by sprouting hair in novel ways and places. No, I mean I have been cultivating the stuff of which Rapunzel and Samson boasted – the hair on your head kind of hair. When I was younger, what with school and finding work and raising a family, I never got much chance to be a hippie. Now in my sixties I am catching up on the Sixties and letting my freak flag fly.

Haven't had a haircut for a year, and the stuff flows down to my shoulders and curls in tendrils at my temples. Most days I wear my hair in a stubby pony tail, gathered at the back of my head in a black plastic band. Originally, I was aiming for a Thomas Jefferson look, a shock of hair tied at the back with a jaunty blue ribbon. But lately I have discovered that my hair has thinned to reveal a gleaming swath of scalp. My Jefferson coiffure has turned into a Ben Franklin.

As Christmas draws near, I peer into the mirror and wonder if I could pass for Santa Claus. There's a slight resemblance despite the fact that the hair is still mostly dark and the gray beard too short to suit the old codger that peeps from Christmas cards. The wrinkles are just right, and the figure is perfect. When I step from the shower I shake like a bowlful of jelly.

Years ago, when my kids were small, I donned a Santa Claus suit for a neighborhood Christmas party and made with the Ho-Ho-Hos while the local youngsters frolicked about the Christmas tree. Long flowing white cotton beard, dashing sock cap, red suit with shiny black belt and pillows to simulate the proper rotundity. I remember how my chin itched and I wondered how men could stand to wear such hair all summer. I pulled up the cotton beard to scratch and thereby created the most pure, innocent Christmas moment of that year. The sight of Santa Claus beardless sent the children into fits of giggles.

The Santa wig embodied a certain time of life, and I discovered that hair provides a sort of history of my evolving Christmas. There's a musty photograph album with a picture of me aged six standing before a sparkling Christmas tree, a happy boy with thick bangs spread on a forehead smooth as angel wings. And later in that album a snapshot of me as a pre-teen, grinning and full of beans, wearing a hand-me-down checkered shirt and spikey hair stiffened with Butch Wax, a precursor of punk rockers. Oh, and let's not forget the Christmas party in the high school year book and my jock's burr cut that made me look like a pro linebacker, except without muscles.

No pictures of it, but I went off to college and adopted a shaggy Beatles-like mop of hair – not because I was faddish but because I was reluctant to spend my beer money on haircuts. Then a few years later the mop disappeared when Uncle Sam seized me and sheared off my hair-do and my personality. When I got Christmas leave from Army boot camp, to visit home before I shipped off to Nam, I thought everyone treated me gingerly because I was in such badass good shape and wearing a snappy uniform. But maybe it was the haircut.

There is no photo of me with a Sonny Bono disco hair-do, wearing a paisley shirt and bell bottoms and a Frito Bandito mustache, hanging peace symbols on an aluminum Christmas tree. But there could have been. The Seventies happened, but I like to think I destroyed all the evidence.

Mid-seventies and children begin to appear in my Christmas photos, munchkins in pajamas and robes hovering in excitement before a scraggly pine tree. Normally I am off camera, the one taking the picture, but occasionally my blurred image haunts the background, a fellow in a dress shirt with rolled-up sleeves. Dad the engineer with a dorky Christmas tie and a Dilbert haircut. The back of my neck would be shaved clean in those days before the AIDS scare. As the years roll by the pictures are much the same, and the children grow taller springing up like corn stalks, and my locks wax gradually longer, from crew cut to polo player to a blow-dried politician's coif. Somewhere in there appears a business executive haircut; it's the same as a regular cut but costs twice as much.

And these days I sport longish hair. I'm not sure what it means. Perhaps I'm trying to get in touch with my feminine side. I have learned that tonsorial splendor is a lot of work. It takes hours each week to wash, rinse, comb, blow dry, shape and tease hair – and that's not counting the rituals beyond my skill set – the weaving, braiding, bleach, hair spray and mousse. Until I let it grow, I never realized how hard it is to maintain a luxuriant head of hair. All I do is clump it at the back and give it a twist and then ensnare it with a band and let it flop – and even that much is a chore. Hair is another name for hassle.

I tolerate the hassle, not to gain appreciation of women's lot, and not to achieve a better imitation of Santa Claus, and not – let's be clear – for the sake of my looks. I think I let my hair flow because it makes me feel free. It makes me feel like I can shake my fist at the sky and cry out, "No, by cracky and dag nab it, I ain't dead yet. I am still changing and learning and growing – if only my hair."

And that's what I wish for you, my friends, after all these Christmases. I wish you the feeling that we are free, that we are able to change, that things are changing, that anything can happen – that oxen might talk on a snowy evening and that a naked baby in a stable might grow up to change the world.

Here's wishing you a Hairy Christmas and a Hirsute New Year!

Gary

Water Like a Stone

[*This year I sent a story about boyhood, not exactly a Christmas story, but still a winter's tale, not exactly a true story, but true enough, not exactly brimming with holiday good cheer, but still something to make us all merry.*]

Dear friends and family,

Winter has lost some of its terror and much of its charm since global warming began to slushify everything. A generation or two ago the Midwestern winter was harsh and long. Winter lasted a full three months and the cold snapped tree limbs and froze milk bottles on the back porch. A dog left in the back yard overnight might freeze to death. Usually before Christmas a few dustings of snow had fallen, and by January the snow had developed muscle and teeth.

Such a snow began falling one January evening years ago and kept falling all night. It covered houses, lawns and streetlights of the small Midwestern town like a sodden woolen blanket. In the morning all over town children gathered restlessly around the breakfast table to munch cereal splashed with milk and listen to the family radio set. They paused breathlessly when the local news announcer interrupted the Arthur Godfrey Show to report that school was closed because of impassable roads. Over spoons loaded with Cheerios, the neighborhood children beamed at each other. They did not shout for joy before their parents, but kept silent, bottling inside themselves the prospect of a day skipping school with the streets and parks and playgrounds swathed in snow. It was a gift from heaven.

Neighborhood boys came out while the snow was still descending. They burst from their houses in the early morning dressed like Russian dolls. After the obligatory snowball fight, which always ended in a melee of silent powdery explosions, and an hour or so of miscellaneous tramping and sledding and clashing in icicle sword fights, they gathered together to plan a construction project. Every year that brought a fine, heavy snowfall they built something different. One year it had been a sledding ramp down Cemetery Hill, with a treacherous run around a clump of headstones which they named "Dead Man's Curve". Once they built a snow fort complete with archer's loop-holes and a hand-made ice box for storing ammunition. This particular snowfall arrived slightly moist and perfect for packing. The quality of the snow inspired them to build a giant snowman.

Traffic was absent, and the small neat front lawns had been trampled during the snowball fight, so the gang of boys built their snowman right in the middle of the street. First the older and stronger Harmon twins rolled a huge hard snowball, as big as they could push, waist high for the base. Then the smaller fellows,

Smitty and Malcolm, rolled a medium snowball as big as a boulder. It took two boys to lift it atop the base. Then the gang's leader, Bill Jenkins, rolled a smaller ball and set it on top for a head. The youngest boy, Lester Penn, begged leftover Christmas candy from his mother. He was lifted up so he could stick licorice squares in the head to form a black toothy smile and two green gumdrops for eyes. Someone found half a tennis ball for a nose and twigs for arms. Someone's mother contributed an old gray fedora and a red scarf to finish the snowman with elegance.

They stood back as a group to inspect their work. It was beautiful, tall as a man, immaculate and glistening in the faint sunlight. It smiled gamely and inanely at the wide, white world. Little Lester Penn said that it should have a name, and so the boys dubbed it "Mr. Frosty."

The boys walked around the thing, admiring it from every angle. At first, they addressed the snowman with solemnity. "Pleased to meet you, Mr. Frosty." "Nice day, isn't, Mr. Frosty? Nice and snowy." Smitty tried a joke. "Hey Mr. Frosty, your head is too big for that hat!" Malcolm chimed in with, "Hey Mr. Frosty, that's a beaut of a nose!"

In the silence following their giggles, they heard a car motor rumbling in the distance. At first the sound meant nothing, just an oddity to hear a car on that snow-muffled morning, but Bill Jenkins spied across the alley, on the other side of the block, Tommy Horsheck in his father's Buick.

That meant trouble. Tommy was a notorious high school bully, older than any of the neighborhood gang by at least four years, the son of the town's only surgeon, and consequently rich and spoiled, and a boy born to raise Hell. He must have talked his father into some form of cabin fever emergency or snowbound fantasy to get the loan of the new Buick on such a foul day.

Nothing moved on the streets but the big black Buick. Tommy was drunk with power. He deliberately fishtailed up the empty street in large lazy arcs. The wheels churned furiously as the car slid sideways from curb to curb, occasionally grazing a mailbox, then whipping around to veer sideways toward the mailbox on the opposite side of the street. The Buick careened up the block opposite and turned the corner to climb to the top of the block where the boys had built their snowman. When it reached the top of the hill, the car slowed to a crawl and then stopped, like a beast sizing up its prey. It sat for a moment, rumbling and then shrieking as Tommy gunned the engine. Slowly it began to roll down the street, picking up speed, its exhaust kicking up a growing plume of snow dust. It headed straight at the snowman.

"Oh no!" the boys' hearts cried. "Tommy! Don't! Tommy! Stop! Look out!"

The Buick barreled down the hill, implacable as demon love. It roared louder and louder as it stooped to the kill. It drove straight into the snowman and smashed it to mush.

76

Tommy Horsheck and his father's Buick skidded back to the center of the street and continued merrily on their way. They coasted through the stop sign at the end of the block and emitted a faint bleat of car horn. The cold breeze brought a whiff of distant, fiendish laughter.

The boys stood on the curb and surveyed the demolished snowman. Half a head, bearing one eye and a comma of licorice drop smile, lay sunk in the gutter snow. A maple twig arm was crushed under tire marks. The base of the snowman's beautiful stout belly was cut off at bumper height, like the foam cut off a glass of beer. All the rest had been obliterated.

"That Tommy Horsheck is a jerk," said Bill Jenkins.

As a group the boys' blood thrilled with the truth of his observation.

A few of the boys bit their lips in anger. Smitty examined the crushed fedora. Malcolm picked up the soiled scarf. Little Lester Penn began to whimper. The snow-muffled air fell silent. Nothing fair and pure remained in the wide, white world.

"We ought to get even," said Bill Jenkins. "We ought to teach that guy a lesson. And come to think of it, I think I know how. Hey, listen, I have an idea."

Under Bill's direction the boys laid out a new construction plan. There was no time to waste, because Tommy Horsheck would return to the scene of his crime, and it had to be finished before he came back. The two biggest boys, the twins Jody and Rudy Harmon, raced up a driveway to the alley. The rest of the boys began gathering snow, armloads and buckets and shovels full of the stuff. In a few minutes Jody and Rudy returned, lugging a huge garbage can of bricks. The brick was left over from Mr. Schmidt's summer project of repairing his backyard incinerator. The can of brick had been sitting in the alley for six months because the city would not pick it up and Mr. Schmidt was too cheap to have it hauled.

"Gosh, this can is heavy as a ton of bricks," said Rudy.

"Well, what do you expect?" said Jody. "Shut up and keep pushing."

The can was so heavy that the whole gang pitched in to haul it down the curb and slide it into place in the middle of the street. They worked like beavers, packing snow into a great ball around the garbage can. They hoisted a medium ball on that and perched a hasty head on that and decorated the whole with bits of tree bark for vest buttons and face. They recovered the misshapen fedora and clapped it jauntily on the snowman's head. Bill Jenkins stuck a tree branch in the torso for an arm and he re-tied the red scarf. The scarf flapped in the breeze like a tiny red flag. The effect, they decided, was irresistible.

And then beautifully, just as they stepped back to survey the new snowman, Tommy

Horsheck's father's Buick peeped over the hill. This time the car did not pause but steadily crept forward, coasting quietly. Then the engine roared and the car lurched into gear. It zoomed down their street, gathering steam, heedless of traffic laws, personal peril, public safety and the good sense God gave a goose. Faster and faster, trailing a sparkling cloud of snow, it plowed toward the gallant little snowman.

"Oh yes!" their hearts cried. "Tommy! Don't stop! Look out!"

The Buick rammed into the brick snowman with a tremendous bang. Headlights exploded, metal snapped and tore, the grill caved in like meringue. The car horn began blaring as the Buick slid to a halt thirty yards down the street, hissing steam. The car roared, screamed, wheezed and then with a cough, fell silent. Its wake was littered with shattered glass, chrome, busted bricks and a bright red ribbon of scarf.

The gang of boys toppled like dominoes flat on their backs in the snow, convulsed and half sick with laughter. Bill Jenkins glanced up to see if Tommy Horsheck was dead or at least bleeding. But he was okay; he was groaning. Smitty was laughing so hard he was crying. Malcolm was holding his sides as though his ribs might fall out.

Tommy Horsheck stumbled out the car door and staggered to the mangled hood holding his head in both hands. He took a few feeble steps toward the boys, as though he might try to take on the whole gang, but the laughter froze him in his tracks. He stared at the wreck of his father's Buick, at the swath of glass splinters and brick rubble. He sank to his knees in the snow and moaned.

The boys left him there. They brushed off snow and headed for their homes and lunch and mothers' steaming mugs of cocoa. They knew they had witnessed something important. There can be justice in this cold world, if only we make it so.

Before they left, very quietly at first and then swelling to shouts, they broke into song. "Bumpitty-bump-bump, bumpitty-bump-bump, look at Frosty go! Bumpitty-bump-bump, bumpitty-bump-bump, overrrr the fields of snowwwww!"

Happy holidays to one and all, and be kind to snowmen,

Gary

Christmas Politics

[*This letter went out in a year when political discourse in America became especially heated and disjointed. Come to think of it, that could be almost any year.*]

Dear friends, family, and my fellow Americans,

After supper on Christmas eve my family would gather in the living room prior to the arrival of Santa Claus and the merry chaos of gift exchange. The kids would be sprawled on the floor before the glittering Christmas tree, playing canasta or Monopoly or Go Fish. The adults would be draped on various motley chairs of our overly-warm jam-packed two-bedroom house.

The talk of the adults usually ranged from the weather (cold) to sports (St. Louis Cardinals) to recipes (egg nog) to work (not much). Eventually and inevitably it ran to politics and a jocular, but not too jocular, battle of wits. Some years the FDR Democrats won, and some years the Eisenhower Republicans won, but every year courtesy and reason went down in ignominious defeat.

Dad would be plopped in a big easy chair, perhaps sipping eggnog, perhaps sweetened with a drop of rum, and he would fire off the first salvo. He would speak, not to any particular person, but with a broad gesture to the world at large.

"This country is going to Hell in a hand-basket."

"Casmer," Mom would say. "Watch your language."

"Well, I mean it. In a hand-basket and no doubt about it. We've been reeling like a drunken sailor ever since Eisenhower got in."

"Oh, baloney, " Aunt Velma would pipe up. She always took the bait. "Look at all the roads he's building."

"Yeah, and the way things are going, nobody will be able to buy a Studebaker to drive on them. Or even a damn Ford."

"Casmer, really."

"And they changed the pledge of allegiance," said Uncle Ernie, sipping his beer and gesturing with a pretzel. "[slurp] The Pledge of Allegiance! Jesus Christ! Is nothing sacred?!"

"Oh, I don't know it's so bad," Uncle Frank would offer, grabbing a handful of peanuts straight from the can. "Look at unemployment. It was bad after The War, and after Korea and all the GI's coming home to no work, but now people got jobs. [chomp] Even my goldbrick brother-in-law."

Aunt Ethel glared at her husband Frank. Everybody knew that her brother had been out of work for a year, and that he drank a bit, and that he just got a temporary job driving a snow-plow. She said nothing, because she hardly ever said anything. She just frowned at her husband and casually dropped cigarette ash on the carpet.

"Sure," Dad said. "There's jobs, but what kind of jobs? And how does Eisenhower pay for them? By raising the national debt, that's how. Millions and billions. That's billions with a 'b'. Borrow today, squander the money on roads and tanks, and then saddle these poor youngsters with debt. These poor kids," and here he swept the air, encompassing with effusive compassion the children and their card games. "These kids will be paying off the debt for Eisenhower's make-work programs until nineteen-seventy!"

"That's true," said Aunt Jenny, fingering the bottom of a Whitman's Sampler chocolate to make sure it contained none of the dreaded maple cream. "But folks [smack] need work."

Uncle Jack chimed in. "That's true too." He glanced around the room to be sure that no one was offended. He really had no interest in politics, other than to vote against Prohibition, but he wanted to sound like an informed citizen. He said, "Don't blame me. I voted for Adlai." When Aunt Jenny winced at this cop-out, Jack retired to the kitchen to freshen his CC and Seven-Up.

Aunt Velma launched a little light artillery. "General Eisenhower is still protecting us. He's got the Commies on the run, and the Mexican wetbacks, and he brought to his administration the best brains in America – Sherman Adams, Henry Cabot Lodge, Richard Nixon."

Uncle Ernie retaliated. "Nixon! Oh, get serious. [slurp] Nixon is a weasel." Around the room the adults nodded in unison. Yes indeed, without a doubt, Nixon, a weasel.

"One thing I really like about Ike," said Uncle Frank, "[chomp] he's a general. He thinks strategy. He's going to make Alaska a state. Make it American and keep the Russians out. Very smart."

"Yeah, sure," said Dad. "Like he kept the Chinese out of Korea. All he did was look the other way, declare Korea a victory, and then turn tail. The Chinese already got Manchuria, and they're headed to Mongolia, mark my word, and then they take Tibet and Indochina and then a weakened Japan and then Hawaii. Next stop: Santa Monica pier!"

All the grownups chuckled at the idea of Chinese troops in square hats riding the Ferris wheel at Santa Monica pier.

"But he's going to make Hawaii a state too, and keep the Red Chinese out," said Uncle Frank. "Eisenhower knows foreign policy. He got Secretary Dulles to pull the French out of Indochina."

"Oh, right," said Dad, his voice dripping with sarcasm. "He pushes the French out of their own country – why do you think they call it French Indochina? Not smart at all. Dulles betrays the French and the British and gives away the Suez Canal. That's lame-brained. He coddles our enemies and insults our friends. Dulles don't know beans."

At this point my brother Bob spoke up. He was home from college, teetering on the edge of adulthood and therefore allowed to squeeze in a word or two in the grownups' conversation. He said, "John Foster Dulles is the Secretary of State. His grandfather was Secretary of State, and his uncle too. And his brother runs the CIA. I'd say that means he knows beans and a lot more."

For a moment, the adults fell silent. They stared at Bob in speechless astonishment. This was a new weapon in the arsenal of after-dinner talk. Information was a formidable weapon.

Dad was flabberghasted. He stared at Bob with a mixture of wonder, admiration and disgust, seeking some way to carry home his point. "Facts!" he shouted. "Here I am trying to save the world, trying to teach these kids what goes on, and here you are citing me facts! Facts don't pertain. Just," – and he looked around the room seeking inspiration because he knew he was painted into a rhetorical corner – "just because facts don't deliver what we need. What we need is the Truth!"

At this point the family erupted. Everybody spoke at once.

"Oh, for pete's sake!" "Oh [slurp] come off it!" "What a [chomp] bunch of hogwash!" "That is ridiculous and you know it!" "Baloney!" "Go Fish!"

85

At five years old and three feet tall, my little sister Lynn was the smallest person in the room, but her voice carried conviction. She was listening intently like all the children, and keeping silent so as not to miss a word, but she grew alarmed at the adult commotion. She searched for something to calm the old folks and get everyone focused on the really important matters. "Everybody, please!" she shouted, her voice cracking a little and her blonde curls bobbing. "Please! Just listen! It's Christmas! And, and, and besides Santa is coming so we should be nice."

And with those words, peace descended like fresh fallen snow. Velma beamed at Frank and Jenny at Ernie, and Mom beamed at Dad and Grandma sighed. For a minute or two there reigned in our home Peace on Earth, Good Will toward Men.

Santa is always coming. Happy holidays!

Gary

Rio Christmas

Dear friends and family,

I am writing this Christmas letter from my hotel room overlooking the tan sand and turquoise waves of the south Atlantic just off Copacabana Beach. Yeah, that's right, I'm spending Christmas in Rio de Janeiro. The day is balmy, palm trees are swaying, the holiday shoppers stroll the streets in thongs and bathing suit wraps. Santa wears shorts. The Rio scene probably sounds appealing to you, stuck as you are in chilly climes and slush. But it's not all that exotic, really. It's just a job.

I find myself stuck in Rio because I'm one of those fellows who does not need to be home for the holidays. I got divorced several years ago, my kids are grown and busy with their own lives, but no grandchildren yet, and so I have no urgent need to gather with friends and family around the yule log. The fellows with young children long fervently to be home for Christmas, and yet somebody needs to stay behind to manage the skeleton crew and keep the project percolating. I volunteered to stay in Rio. I figured, might as well help the team, and besides, I'm enjoying the work and learning lots about daily life and holiday happenings in the Southern Hemisphere.

The project is blazing trails. Our client is Telemar, the Brazilian equivalent of AT&T, the largest telephone company in the southern hemisphere. With the advent of cell phones, the telcos down here are expanding at break-neck speed. The demand for cellphone service far exceeds the supply and so we are laying down fiber-optic cables and erecting cell towers and building out network control rooms as fast as we can. Budget is effectively unlimited, says Telemar, and we consultants rejoice in it. There's something exhilarating about working a project where we can network, network, network full speed ahead and never mind the cost.

The trouble is, as my boss puts it, "It's a beautiful country, but nothing works." Brazil remains a third-world country. Laying down modern telecommunications on a medieval infrastructure presents enormous challenges. Since telephone poles were mostly never erected, telephone lines are strung from building to building, and they intersect typically in a mare's nest of tangled wires overhead. Solution is simple – go wireless everywhere. But to put up cellphone towers, you need electrical power and high capacity links from station to station, and while we run those wires in America through existing storm sewers, Rio lacks storm sewers and even waste sewers, so we jackhammer through the charming mosaic sidewalks to lay down fiber cables and the result is everywhere sidewalks churned into rubble. Walking around Rio is like walking a battlefield, skirting open pits and piles of bricks and stones. The people of Rio seem unconcerned by the mess and inconvenience, being accustomed to happy chaos.

I've been down here about two months now, and getting into a routine. The men in our crew — there are no women among the engineers on this project — stay at a luxury hotel off Copacabana. The rooms are spacious, well-appointed and pleasantly aired by sea breezes, but occasionally we have to walk up six sweltering flights because the elevator is broken. Rio is beautiful but nothing works. Monday mornings my walk to our offices includes a stop to drop off laundry – the hotel service is pricey – and I sip coffee standing at a sidewalk bar with the Cariocas (natives). I manage in my pidgin Portuguese to order passion fruit pastry and coffee laced with warm milk. The local people are civil but they tend to ignore me because I don't speak the language. I am tolerated but not welcomed, like a kangaroo standing at the coffee bar. My six-block walk to work, skirting trenches in the sidewalks, takes me past restaurants, dentist offices, drug stores, and clean, kempt professional office buildings. Everywhere poor people litter the streets. In shaded alleyways stand beggars, men hawking cocoanut water, whores, ragged natives selling wood carvings and, for all I know, pirates fleeing scurvy.

When it's December in Rio, things are as Christmasy as Kansas in August. Daytime temperatures reach into the nineties, and direct sunlight feels like a blast furnace. No sleigh rides but plenty of beach volleyball. No Christmas carols over loud speakers but patches of lilting samba music drifting from sidewalk cafes. The entrance to fancy Ipanema Beach hotels sports palm tree trunks wound with little green lights. Billboards along the Avenida Atlantica promote Jim Carrey as The Grinch and also delicious air conditioning. The shopping mall at Rio Sul sprouted thousands of giant gold balls and tinsel dangling from the ceiling. Of course, it's Rio and nothing works very well. I watched a huge gold plastic ornament fall from the vaulted mall ceiling down to the escalator and bonk a shopper on the head. The shopper looked up casually, as though giant ornaments fall as commonly as acorns. The huge golden ball fell to the floor and was trampled in the steady stream of earnest shoppers. Angels we have heard on high.

Last night I saw a beautiful slice of Rio Christmas. A guy from the client firm, perhaps my first Brazilian friend, Gustavo, invited me to dinner. (Well, actually, the economics of it are a bit more complicated than that, since I picked up the tab, and I will expense it to his company, the big Brazilian telco, Telemar, and of course Telemar will recoup the dinner bill as expenses against their tax burden, or perhaps costs rolled into their pricing model, so that neither of us paid for anything, but rather we the people, you the people, the taxpayers and consumers of Brazil and all those affected by their pocketbooks, in other words everyone bought our dinners last night. That's how we do business. Thank you very much.)

Gustavo and I sat down to dinner at one of his favorite restaurants, a place called Moustarda in the city section known as Lagoa. The restaurant features various dishes prepared with exotic mustards, and the tables have lazy-susan trays loaded with herb and red wine mustard and the like, to be sampled with the warm cheese rolls served before the meal. The restaurant walls were painted mustard yellow, and the furniture was green mustard fabric threaded with gold. Frank Lloyd Wright would have loved the place.

So, as I said, we sat down to dinner. (My goodness, if these digressions go on much longer I will simply starve.) We were lucky enough to get a table on the veranda, in the open air and overlooking a large expanse of sleek black lake (lagoa). Wafted over the water came the faint sounds of a symphony concert being held on the other side of the lake. I could just barely make out the music; possibly it was Waltz of the Flowers from Tchaikovsky's *Nutcracker Suite*. And then, somewhere between the grouper *carpaccio* and the fillet Dijon, fireworks erupted over the lake, and sputtering firecrackers (which Gustavo calls "bangers"), and then slowly into view floated an immense electric Christmas tree, a shimmering tower of silver lights in the shape of a perfect fir. Gustavo explained that this year the tree had been extended, now at least 50 meters high, because last year another community claimed that it had the world's tallest Christmas tree at 45 meters, and the mayor of Rio had vowed not to be outdone. The tree was a huge tower of meshed wire studded with programmable lights, with flood lights at the base that could turn the thing green one moment, blue the next, or a tawny gold that nicely off set the white or blue twinkle lights that formed the metal fir branches. The whole thing was mounted on a floating island that Gustavo claimed was manned by a boat pilot and two computer technicians. When all the lights went off, along about the *crème brulee*, the tree became a huge black silhouette, drifting in a glistening black lake, set against the distant lights of houses in the hills, framed by the great shadow of Corcovado mountain with its lighted statue of Christ Redeemer overlooking the city. A lovely view and dinner on the expense account. Thank you very much.

    Gustavo and I discussed over dinner the economics of Brazil. He is an amateur historian, I guess, even though he works as a translator/systems analyst by daylight. We had been discussing the Vietnam War, the American election (which all

Brazilians seem to follow avidly), his mosquito-ridden two months touring the Amazon jungle, and his goofy conviction that Hitler was a liberal – because, like Marx, he advocated an end to tariffs and a nearly laissez-faire business climate. When we got to economics, Gustavo explained that much of the society I see today is radically different from the one he grew up in. He was a boy of eleven during the Vietnam era, and has only a vague idea of the turmoil that shook America in the sixties. In his youth, the American-backed military junta seized Brazil (1964), and there was a Great Oppression, and he remembers riots in the streets and a cousin who left to join guerilla forces in the mountains and was killed in gunfire. The modern, cosmopolitan, ostensibly capitalist, sort of democratic society which we see today is something that happened only in his middle age. As a young man he was used to tales of military takeover of newspapers, people being "disappeared" when they protested rigged elections, scandals that permitted radioactive beef to be imported from Europe, teargas disrupting parades, fixed courts and 20 per cent inflation per month. And always the poor were hungry in this phenomenally rich agricultural country.

I mentioned the throngs of beggars in the streets, even along the ritzy Ipanema. Gustavo had no way to explain the poor. He just shrugged his shoulders and frowned in that Latin way, as if to say, *"Quien sabe?"* And I reflected on my own country and the great and probably growing disparity between rich and poor in the good old USA. I do not know what to do about America any more than Gustavo knows what to do about Brazil. A clue to what we must do comes from an incident a month ago, on Thanksgiving.

I flew back to Chicago to catch up on mail and bills and to enjoy a respite from the overbearing sunshine of Brazil. It had been a pleasant Thanksgiving Day. I had taken my friend Mary and my son Nathan to a fancy restaurant, The Palm at Swisshotel, and we had the traditional turkey dinner in an elegant setting. Crisp white table linen, courteous waiters, gleaming silver. And then we went to a 3-D super movie and hung out at the Navy Pier Amusement Park, and by the time we drove home it was dark. After we parked behind my building, walking up to the back door, I noticed a disheveled black man rummaging in the dumpster in the alley. I hustled Mary indoors and then I walked to the closet to take off my coat, frowning, vaguely ashamed that such an unsightly bum should intrude upon our holiday evening. When I returned to the kitchen, the back door was open and Mary was gone. I walked out on the porch stoop to see Mary in the alley, carrying white plastic bags she had taken from the refrigerator, the excess food, the doggie bags we had retrieved from an excellent Vietnamese dinner the night before. She gave the poor black man the doggie bags, and he thanked her, and I suppose he took home to his family a Thanksgiving dinner of ginger duck and curry shrimp. When Mary returned to the kitchen, she was crying.

"We have so much," she said, "and he has so little."

Immediately I was flooded with shame – because I had dismissed the creature at the back door as a nuisance – and Mary had seen a needy human being. There it was Thanksgiving Day, and I had experienced nothing really special all day, just pleasant food and frolic, until that moment of Mary's easy, instant, human gesture. I thought what a privileged and lucky fellow I am, to have friends who can show me how to be a better human being. Thank you very much.

I guess I should sign off this letter and get back to work. Power to the client's computer main control room failed again, and the Unix servers all crashed, and the crew cannot locate the reboot tapes, and people are paging me again. Sigh. But we're still in Beta test, not production, and it's still Christmas season, so first, another anecdote about Rio.

My erudite Brazilian friend Gustavo invited me to his home about a week after Thanksgiving. It was, I realized then and more so now, an unusual gesture and an honor. Gustavo lived for a couple years in Los Angeles. He speaks four languages. He provides invaluable translation and technical assistance to our project, and I help him in his role as Telemar corporate liaison by telling him selective truths about the progress (or lack thereof) of our project. We hit it off, and he invited me to drop by for breakfast on a Saturday morning.

A short taxi ride from my hotel, Gustavo's home shone in the morning sun like a hacienda, presenting a large white stucco split level with blue shutters on a quiet street that backed up to *Aterro do Brigadeiro Eduardo Gomes*, or Flamengo Park. The park is the largest tract of jungle located within city limits anywhere in the world, located between the Copacabana and downtown Rio. Gustvo's wife, a pretty middle-aged woman with strikingly white teeth, greeted me at the gate and led me past a small tile entryway with a shaded koi pond. She spoke very little and apologized for her English, but I liked her instantly, her kind eyes and megawatt smile. We walked straight through the house onto a screened porch at the back where Gustavo sat at a wicker table set with gleaming china and silverware. The porch hung out near a patch of jungle sporting palm trees, strangler figs, and lianas draped from tree limb to limb like a set from a Tarzan movie. Breakfast was the sort of modified European fare typical of Brazil – rolls and butter, thin-sliced cheese, steaming coffee and numerous fruit plates including papaya, passion fruit, bananas and berries. The talk was pleasant, with Gustavo growing expansive and animated there in the security of his own home.

Just as the party was breaking up and I was about to make my thanks and farewell, a troop of monkeys appeared in the trees not far off the porch. They screeched and grunted, making quite a racket. They hopped through the trees on scrawny, hairy black limbs flashing in the morning sun, waving long prehensile tails. Gustavo shouted at them, doubtless a hearty Portuguese curse, and he tried to hustle me off the porch, explaining that monkeys were dirty animals and a nuisance – the way I consider squirrels back home a nuisance. But I lingered a few moments in wonder. I mean, yes they were only neighborhood pests, but how often do you have a monkey parade at breakfast?

Really now, that is enough about Christmas in Rio de Janeiro. I should head back to the office. I started this letter in a jocular mood, off-handedly trying to make you feel envious of lucky me basking in the sun while you poor Norte Americanos shiver in the cold, but I suspect that I have lingered over this letter because it's a way to summon up something warmer still. The Christmas spirit, for me, radiates its own kind of warmth. This place is familiar in many ways, with Christmas trappings and twinkling lights, and even the ragged poor in the shadows, but a holiday in the heat only sharpens the pangs of alienation. I miss you folks and I hope you miss me too. Wish I could send you warm breezes from the beach at Ipanema, but I'll content myself with sending warm thoughts.

    Feliz Natal, Merry Christmas

    Gary

Yule Haiku

Dear friends,

This year just some poetry. You probably know about haiku, a Japanese poetry form consisting of three brief, evocative lines in a fixed format of 5 syllables, then 7 syllables, then 5 syllables again. I find it oddly liberating to compose to such a confining format. There are infinite ways to say a thing, and one infinity is large as another.

Trembling starry sky
Contains a hopeful silence
You can hear Christmas

A deer's mincing steps
Pierce the crust of moonlit snow
Nature holds its breath

Children laughing shout
Huzzah for the sledding hill
And never return

Less decoration
Than emblem of defiance
Aluminum tree

She donates wool coats

And mittens to warm the poor
Stops and hugs herself

Raggedy Ann doll
Missing arm and button eye
What survives is love

Apples and oranges
Float in steaming cider punch
Kindness comes in cups

Merry Christmas friends/and may the season bring you/joy in the New Year,

Gary

Have Yourself a Merry Quantum Christmas

[This letter went out last year or the year before, I'm not sure. I don't keep track of dates very well. But the letter is reasonably contemporaneous, and yet it will soon seem outdated, because it deals with technology, and the pace of change in technology is staggering. I can hardly imagine my grandfather's life, the time before airplanes, and my grandchildren will wonder why I bothered to learn handwriting. But some things, I hope, will not change for a long, long time.]

Dear Humans,

Lately I've been reading about Artificial Intelligence and the coming of quantum computing, photonics, and vast neural networks which will one day (soon) achieve the complexity of the human brain and so achieve consciousness. In a flash these sentient machines will surpass mere human understanding, grasping all branches of mathematics with never an error in calculation, understanding natural languages and so digesting all human history, philosophy and literature in a matter of minutes, building impeccably precise decision-trees and exploring in nanoseconds a billion-billion possibilities in fuzzy logic yielding lightning fast feedback and comprehension of truth, justice and all known knowledge. Here and now, in our lifetimes, we can see the limitations of the merely human mind and our inevitable devolution into servants and cyborgs, eventually becoming helpless as dodo birds and similarly extinct.

But then I think about Christmas, and I'm not so sure. That's right, you heard right, jolly old Christmas — endearing story of a child newborn, transmuted winter solstice, schoolchild's reprieve and parent's reverie. You may think of it as a pleasant legend, or the Holy made human, or perhaps just a godsend to retailers everywhere, but I urge you to think again. Christmas — or for that matter, Hanukkah, Kwanzaa, and all such holidays — point to what separates us from mechanical minds. Christmas embodies those graces uniquely, irreducibly and irreplaceably human.

Celebrations like Christmas — or Diwali or Omisoka for that matter — invite us to take a holiday from rationality. Christmas from the get-go has defied reason. It is a time of miracles — from the big miracle of Messiah to the homely miracle of King Wenceslas schlepping through slush. Christmas began with a whopping good story of a miraculous birth, complete with a beacon star and singing angels, and then over time people embroidered the tale with talking donkeys and drumming shepherd boys, and then they added flying reindeer, a talking snowman, singing chipmunks and Snoopy slapping up Christmas lights on his dog house. Hah! A decorated dog house! I'd like to see AI invent something as goofy as that.

Irrationality incarnate visited me as a child in the form of Santa Claus. Santa was a sort of super hero, possessed of virtues and abilities beyond all ordinary experience. He could fly through the air like Superman, commanding a sort of Batmobile loaded with a bottomless sack of toys. He could transform himself from a fur-clad fat man into a wisp of smoke that could slip down a chimney. He could stop time each Christmas Eve and, at his leisure, visit every home on Earth in one night, bringing to good children (and let's face it, we were all good children) toys and joys and peppermint.

And why did Santa do all that? There was no profit in it, no survival advantage, no tax break. It simply didn't stand to reason. Yet he came year after year out of love, and not just any kind of love, but the most unworldly, irrational kind: unconditional love. Saint Nick loved little children – not his own children, but all children, any child, even you. No matter who you were, no matter what remote speck of the planet you inhabited, no matter how dire the household finances, somehow Santa would find you and find a way to show that you were loved. Human minds find that behavior delightful and believable. Computers would not get it. Compassion does not compute.

Years ago, people lacked a vocabulary for AI. We had sci-fi of course, but we dreamed of thinking machines as bumbling servants, like the tubby robot in the 60's TV series "Lost in Space". Robbie the Robot looked like a Hoover vacuum on a Segway, outfitted with whirling mag-tapes and meaningless blinking lights. It talked funny, in a sort of languid drone, like Jeremy Irons heavily sedated. It bumped into things and made comical mistakes and in general resembled a puppy on wheels. But then came HAL the killer computer in *2001: A Space Odyssey*, and things would never be the same. Computers became dangerous in *War Games*; robots became competition in *Terminator*, and loving, graceful machine minds took over the world in *AI*.

Artificial Intelligence can seem just as irrational and unpredictable as people. Computers can generate quasi-random numbers and thereby simulate wandering thoughts, errors and hunches. But always underneath the simulation lies an intricate web of logic, a rigorous algorithm, ineluctable rulesets. Underneath human thought lies – who knows – a sublime glimpse of starlight and an urge to pee.

I remember those heady days in the 1970's when I discovered computers and the power of mechanical "thought". I taught myself to program and studied algorithms and imagined that truly the world was entering a new age of sweetness and light. We would eliminate repetitive drudgery in factories, we would establish world-wide communications and put a college education on every street corner, we would command thinking machines to till fields, sail ships, manage markets and thereby usher in a new age of prosperity and leisure and happiness for all humankind.

One early Christmas morning in those years, sipping coffee in my bathrobe and watching my children charge the Christmas tree to tear into stacks of presents, I mused on what technology was bringing into their innocent world. Was the Information Revolution a gift from some benevolent Santa Claus, or was it more sinister? It took humanity 100,000 years to go from eating ants on a stick to building a bonfire, and another ten thousand years to go from baked boar to bronze and glass. It took only a lifetime for IT to go from punch cards to calculators to mainframes to cellphones and ubiquitous computing. And the pace was accelerating. Information technology was no act of unconditional love, but rather like mischief from the *Sorcerer's Apprentice.* Machines might be destined to rule us. My progeny might not be carbon-based, but rather silicon-based sentient creatures. But if so, something infinitely precious would be lost.

Not all knowledge can be digitized. Can a computer ever know, as a mother does, what secret wish rests in the heart of her child? Is it a satin doll, a wooden sled, a glass unicorn? The fastest computer, equipped with hypersensitive sound and infrared detectors, would make at best an optimized guess. But a mother would know.

Not all decisions need to be rational, and not all actions need to be efficient. The world we should be building will have room for ideas as loopy as a decorated dog house; it will have a time for frivolity and folly and jollity galore; it will have room for imagination, a place for cakes and ale; it will contain not only justice but also mercy; it will preserve the impossible, impractical and yet profoundly desirable message of Christmas:

Peace on Earth, Good Will to All!

Happy holidays, compute your blessings,

Gary

Snow Blue

[This letter went out perhaps around 2012 or 2013. But most of the action comes from 1953 or so. A Christmas letter usually contains the latest family news, but I think it ought sometimes to contain old times too. The one informs the other.]

Dear Friends and Family,

We took up watercolor painting this summer. In August Ellen and I trucked up to Ephraim, Wisconsin for a week of painting lessons. We painted every morning and part of every afternoon, with time left for swimming and mo-ped rides and fish boils. Our instructor taught us beginner things like how to hold a brush and how to how to mix colors and how to paint a wash that spread a lovely graduated smear of pigment across the toothed surface of the paper. We thrilled to watch his deft hands sweep over the paper and, with a subtle brushstroke or a flick of the wrist, turn a blank expanse into a mountain range or a lush forest or a sunset.

I got pretty good at painting the side of a barn. I learned to use a big flat brush to apply a slab of barn red, then a few square dabs of violet for windows, then a wash of burnt umber for the roof and then to finish it off with squiggles to represent prairie grass. I liked to stand back from the paper to admire my work, feeling I imagine like God felt on the Seventh Day.

We have continued painting off and on through the autumn and into early winter. We have discovered that the palette changes with the seasons. The bright light of summer calls for bright colors, chrome yellow and cadmium red, while the dim light of autumn veers into yellow ochre and alizarin crimson the color of dried blood. The winter light is cooler still, and cerulean and cobalt and prussian blues dominate the palette. To my surprise I discovered that a watercolor painting presents snow as something not quite white. Snow doesn't look right if it consists of plain white. A faint blue suggests the bulge of a snow bank, and a dark blue creates shadows of footprints on a snowy path. The bare white paper may work to represent a glint of sunlight on icicles, but the mounds and masses call for a mix of cerulean blue and payne's gray that I call snow blue.

And that's the great thing about painting. Not the result. The result is seldom artful, seldom gorgeous, a far cry from beautiful or even convincing. The process itself is the reward. The effort to get a line perfectly upright and subtly shaded can absorb the self, and the painter floats in a tranquil and blissful state of abnegation. One learns really to look at things, because reproducing an image means going beyond the concept of the thing and seeing the actuality. The wheel of a car is conceptually a circle, but when you look at it from an angle, the shape is an ellipse. Conceptually snow is white, but on close examination snow in daylight contains the color of the sky and the snowman's five-o'clock shadow. What you see exceeds the abstraction; the actual reflects a thousand impressions combined.

While painting a snow scene this winter, I got to thinking about a particular snow that fell on my home town many years ago. The thick, slow snowfall settled on the town like a down quilt. My brother Jim and I, being the only kids home at the time, rushed breathlessly into the hushed fluffy landscape. We tramped in the front yard just to see our footprints.

Almost immediately Jim hit me with a barrage of snowballs, he being elder and a hellion and me being younger and his natural prey. That's the way it was with my brother. He was always bullying me, punching me or dunking me in the community swimming pool or knocking me down on the clay baseball infield. Maybe it was because I was the nosey and noisy kid brother, or maybe that was his bumptious idea of good fun. He pelted me with snowballs and for good measure dumped icy snow down my collar. I sputtered, as usual, and fought back and got my face shoved in the snow, as usual, and I found myself with a bloody nose. The sight of my blood made me cry, and I despised the hot tears more than the cold snow down my back. I hated my brother with the pure hot hatred of childish indignation. I resolved to hate him forever. We fell silent only when we were both panting and sweaty from the exertion.

Jim said to pipe down and to put snow on the back of my neck to stop the bleeding. I thought he was teasing me because the cold snow surely ought to be applied to my sore nose. But I followed his directions and clamped a lump of snow on the back of my neck, and sure enough, the bleeding stopped. Jim said to wipe my nose and he would teach me to make a snow angel. We lay in the snow and spread our legs wide to form the indentation of the angel's robe. We swept our arms in great arcs to make angels' wings. Then we stood back to admire the blue silhouettes. We returned to the warmth of the kitchen for bowls of steaming oatmeal, chattering like sparrows at a bird feeder.

After breakfast we heard whooping from the neighbor's yard and knew that meant trouble. The Dewar brothers next door had discovered the snowfall. The Dewars were demons in down jackets – loud, fierce and deadly accurate with snowballs. The big Dewar, Cal, was not so bad. He might steal our tomatoes or hide our newspaper, but mostly he ignored us. He was in high school and had better things to do. But the little Dewar, Francis, scared me. He liked to play with matches, and once he stuck a needle through the callus on his palm just to show off. While sitting on the Dewar's porch one hot summer day,

Francis shared with me his latest idea of fun. He had a plan, he said, to catch two stray cats and tie their tails together and then sling them over a clothes line and watch them claw out each other's guts. I shuddered in fascination at the workings of Francis' mind. He probably never actually acted on the plan – not due to clemency, but due to a total lack of gullible stray cats.

We knew that the Dewars would ruin anything we did. If we built a sled ramp, they would flatten it, and if we built a snowman, they would smash it to smithereens. The moment we peeped out the back door, they would rain snowballs on our heads. Jim said that our only hope was to build a snow fort.

I thought the snow fort was another of Jim's dumb ideas, that we lacked the time and know-how to build it, but I followed him to the smooth white expanse of the back yard. Jim carried with him the small steel pan used to boil oatmeal. We tromped a flat spot in the corner of the yard to make a solid foundation. Jim sank the pan into a patch that sparkled and pulled it up brimming with packed snow. He set the pan on the flat spot, thumped the top and out popped a perfect cylindrical brick of snow. Quickly he got another load in the pan and deposited another brick, and then another and another. I packed the chinks with moist, gooey snow. We speculated on how the fort would thwart the Dewars, where they might find an angle to attack us, how high the walls must be to block a Dewar fastball.

I was amazed to see the snow fort rise so quickly. I mean, come on, it was Jim's idea. My big goof of a big brother. Look at him, one earmuff on his ear and the other curled around his neck, his hatless head dusted white with snow, his battered tennis shoes leaking snow melt on his thin socks, and him happy as a lark and singing a Christmas carol. I had always thought of Jim as a guy with beans for brains, and yet there he was, a genius, a Leonardo of snow.

When the fort walls were eye high, and a handy spy hole cut in the center and a good supply of baseball-sized snowballs stocked on the floor for ammo, Jim said I should go in the house. He noticed that I had lost my mittens and my hands were blue from the cold. A few minutes later Jim joined me in the kitchen. He stood on the hot air register while his feet thawed and his socks steamed. I sipped a mug of tea and luxuriated in the smell of baking brownies.

I wondered aloud what there was for snacks. Mom suggested that we make a batch of snow ice cream, and I thought: snow ice cream? Is that for real? Is that like Nail Soup, or can a person really make ice cream from snow? Mom instructed us to fetch a pan of clean snow and so we returned to the back yard, found an untouched spot and scraped off the top layer, the stuff that might contain grit and Strontium-90. We carried the fresh snow to the kitchen where Mom added a couple of scoops of sugar and a dollop of milk and two drops of vanilla. She stirred the concoction so that the sugar dissolved into the lump of snow and the milk leaped into the flakey interstices. The first spoonful was delicious.

Jim said it was almost perfect but it lacked something. He took down a pack of food coloring, four bottles in all, red, yellow, blue and green. After a momentary debate we settled on blue. Jim stirred a few drops into the pan, and then a few more, and the dye spread in swirls and turned the mixture the color of cornflowers. It took on the fragrance of lilacs, the texture of passion fruit, and the tang of blueberries.

I don't remember if we ever returned to the snow fort. I don't remember if the Dewars clobbered us or we clobbered them, or even if we met on the battlefield. I don't remember if we ate the brownies or what I got for Christmas or whatever happened to my mittens.

What I remember is thinking that people are never pure black or pure white, that my brother contained cruelty and kindness, foolishness and sagacity, a mix of a thousand virtues and vices combined. And that snow ice cream tastes a hundred times better when it is blue.

Happy Holidays!

Gary

Wintertime

[Not every Christmas is merry, and not every New Year is happy. The suicide rate climbs like a skyrocket in December. Yuletide celebrations and the bustling oblivious crowd make a cruel contrast for those outside in the cold, the homeless, the hungry, the sickly, the lonely. And despite our fleeting good intentions, a new coat, a warm meal and a safe place to sleep tonight – these are not enough. Some folks think, 'All I want for Christmas is somebody else's life.']

Dear friends and family,

Ugh, it's almost Christmas and the house is drafty and the kids are driving me crazy and the furnace is acting up and shopping is a zoo and whose idea was it to have Christmas in December? With apologies to Gershwin, the ditty below should be sung 'slow and mournful':

Wintertime

And the weather is freezin'.

Bears are sleepin'

And the snow drifts are high

Well your Daddy's sick

And your Ma has lumbago.

So cry little baby,

Yeah, go ahead and cry.

Wishing you and yours a happy holiday, or at least a speedy recovery from same,

Gary

Craft Hall Christmas

[Some Christmases are great — all peppermint candy canes and jingling silver bells — and some Christmases are not so hot. There's a value in remembering a mediocre, a bad, even a terrible Christmas, because the one clarifies the other, the way a pinch of salt sharpens the sweet. Consider, for example, the way Christmas staggered my home town the year of the strike.]

Dear friends, family, comrades,

Ours was a refinery town and a union stronghold. We had three refineries — the big complex of the Shell Oil Refinery off Highway 111, and a sprawling Standard Oil Refinery next to that, and south of both those squatted the holding tanks and intricate giant tubing of a smaller plant, Sinclair Petroleum. The refineries ran day and night. From my bedroom window, the horizon was dotted with towers bearing aircraft warning lights and flares from refinery waste burn-off. I was about ten years old before it occurred to me that not every town had a southern night sky colored purple streaked with orange.

At times when the wind blew up from the south, the air stank of diesel fumes and sulfur. Visitors to the town would step out of their cars, sniff, and say, "What is that smell?" Townsfolk would smile and answer, "That's money!"

Nearly half the town worked at the refineries or associated businesses. Not every workman belonged to a union, but most refinery employees and all the skilled trades consisted of organized labor. My father was a construction electrician out of the International Brotherhood of Electrical Workers, Local #649 out of Alton, Illinois. He went to work at the union right after high school. He worked his way up from Apprentice to Wireman to Craftsman to Master Craftsman. He worked all over the area, helping build shopping centers, suburban housing, hydroelectric dams and machinery at the refineries. When the refineries were not hiring, he would travel to places like Joliet, Carbondale and even Billings, Montana – if he was lucky enough to find work out of town.

The people in the union thought of their vocation as "the trades" or "the craft" – something like the guilds of the Middle Ages. They called their meeting place, a hulking brick building in nearby Edwardsville, the Craft Hall, or more commonly, just "Craft". Union members were proud of their association and their work. They found in the union not only employment, but something more, a sense of security and comradeship and significance. Dad liked to say, "You enjoy your weekends? Thank the union!"

For working men (and in those days there were no women electricians), the union was much more than a place to find a job. It was a way of life, a sort of brotherly club. Union members gathered at Craft Hall to discuss wages and strikes, but also to talk Cardinals baseball and the price of onions. The whole family partook of social life at the Craft. Union members held a Valentine's Day Dance and a Halloween costume party and each summer a big picnic, with sack races and apple bobbing and whistles for the kids. They organized a fish fry and cake walk and raffles to raise money for the old and the sick.

The year the unions went on strike, they nearly broke the back of our small town. I was too young at the time to understand the issues – wages probably, and working conditions possibly, since refineries were notoriously dangerous places to make a living. The crane operators went on strike first, something about overtime pay. Then the pipefitters joined them in sympathy, and when management stiffed them, the plumbers and teamsters and other trades joined in solidarity, and then management really dug in their heels and things turned ugly. The plants shut down with only skeleton crews, and the men who crossed picket lines to attend the machinery were reviled as "scabs". Half the town missed paychecks, and the strike dragged on and on while folks cut back on vacations and roast beef and movies. After five or six months, families were eating just beans for dinner and nobody was buying cars or furniture. The men drank too much and the women worried aloud as Christmas rolled around.

The Christmas celebration at Craft Hall usually cheered the family with the promise of fun and good food and music. The year of the strike in particular, it would be good to get way from things, good to get away from glum neighbors, the sour atmosphere of families struggling to make ends meet, an idled father grumpily reading the newspaper from the sofa, a mother scrimping meals from macaroni and leftovers. I was nine years old and oblivious to the larger social issues, but I knew something was wrong. The Boy Scouts cancelled the annual sale of Christmas trees in the Kroger Grocery parking lot. Hauling out trees and shaking off the ice pellets and trimming lower branches was a rite of the season, and I missed it. Adults, I said to myself, are a great mystery, and sometimes amazingly thick-witted.

The precise location of Craft Hall eludes me because we travelled there before I learned to drive a car. That's childhood for you – geography remains vague when you cannot see the road. I usually sat between siblings in the back seat of our old Chevy station wagon, wrangling with my brother or pestering my sister or nose buried in a comic book. After a restless half hour squeezed in the back seat, the family decamped at Craft Hall like the Visigoths invading Rome. The place might have been a renovated church, or an abandoned Masonic lodge, or some such civic white elephant, but to me it was magnificent and huge as a warehouse. The Craft had imposing wide concrete steps leading up to a Greco-Roman façade on a red brick building. Entering the massive doors, we came upon a coat room, a foyer with a dusty chandelier, a hallway lined with photos of union big shots patting each other on the back, and then a spacious grand ballroom. Usually the great room would be set with rows of folding chairs for the business meeting, but at Christmas the ballroom was empty except for a brightly-lit Christmas tree plunked down in the center of everything. The tree had been erected and lighted by a bunch of electricians, so naturally the tree lights were slapped up with a frayed extension cord and a plug converter. Beneath the tree lay a trove of gift-wrapped packages.

Off to one side of the great room stood the "billiard room" – called that because calling it a "pool room" suggested disreputable goings-on such as festered on the shady side of town in dark alleys and ratty pool parlors. So far as I know, no one ever played billiards there. The men shot pool games of Rotation or Eight-ball. We kids would glance in passing at the men assembled around the table, smoking and drinking and chatting. We liked the sound of their deep voices, the cackling laughter, the click of pool balls, and the rumble of balls rolling down the felt-covered slate surface. After the game broke up and the men moved to the business meeting, we boys pretended to shoot pool by shoving the leftover cue ball toward the leather-netted pockets.

At the back of the great room stood a small stage, suitable for a speaker from a lectern, or a magician without assistant, or a church lady warbling show tunes. The stage was big enough for a duet but not a barbershop quartet. At the rear of the stage sat an upright piano and swivel stool. When no one was looking, the girls would clamber up to the piano to bang out "Turkey in the Straw" or "Heart and Soul". The boys turned the piano stool into a merry-go-round. One memorable evening a gray-haired lady commandeered the piano and called for silence. Feelingly she stroked the keys and played while the crowd stood, placed hands on hearts and sang "America the Beautiful". The final chords hung in the air like spirits from a lost world.

The annual Christmas party always seemed a little bizarre. It wasn't really Christmas (that was at home, in the bosom of family and friends) and yet it was sort of Christmas, full of grownups yammering and drinking too much and children racing through hallways in excitement. We ate a common meal, seated at long folding tables covered with paper tablecloths, with everyone jabbering at once and the ladies of the Craft Auxiliary popping out of the kitchen to be sure that everyone got plenty to eat and that the children were behaving. The ladies dried their hands on dish towels and beamed at the noisy crowd. At the end of the meal the crowd begged them to come away from the dishes to receive a hearty round of applause.

The Christmas party kicked off with the entrance of Santa Claus. By tradition, the local union Business Manager played Santa Claus, wearing a red suit, fake whiskers and a stocking cap that covered his shiny Brylcreamed hair. As I recall, Santa from ten feet away smelled of whiskey. Each kid sat at Santa's feet and told him (and thereby his parents) of his deepest wish for a Christmas gift. When I approached Santa, I intended to ask for a magic cape like Mandrake the Magician's, but at the last moment I felt foolish asking for a girlish thing like a cape, so I asked Santa for a chemistry set. (Yes, you're right, cowardice makes fools of us all. As Shakespeare might have said, "Oh, what a candy-ass, wuss and chicken-shit am I.")

Speeches were made, carols were sung, dishes put away while all the kids grew impatient awaiting the communal melee of gift-giving. Usually the gifts were splendid – life-like dolls and racing cars and cap pistols gleaming in sequined holsters. One year the son of the Craftsman of the Year got a shiny new Schwinn bicycle. But this year, the year of the strike, the booty was disappointing. Santa passed out a package for each child, some marked "B" for boys and some marked "G" for girls. We ripped off the wrapping paper to discover simple playthings – notebook paper and pencil, hair ribbons, a tin box of watercolors. Boys got marbles or paddle-ball kits; girls got jacks or jump ropes. Nothing big, nothing fancy, nothing expensive. The strike came home to us children then, that it was for real, and that even Christmas must suffer. The kids sagged briefly and then smiled bravely, as the crowd grew quiet and the adults looked down at their shoes and fidgeted. The Christmas party lurched like a carousel going over a waterfall.

One of the men, maybe it was my Dad, broke the mood by shouting, "Hells bells, jingle bells, let's get this party rolling! Everybody, music, let's dance!"

Folks cleared the floor of long tables and folding chairs and someone fired up the PA system with old-fogey music. Our parents grabbed partners and began dancing, fox trot and waltzes and boogey-woogey. My Mom loved any music by Glenn Miller, and when swing music floated from the overhead speakers, she dashed to the dance floor and shimmered in the light of green and blue and red tree lights. This particular evening at the Christmas party, when the music slowed, she grabbed my small hand and dragged me to the dance floor. I was, what, nine years old, a head shorter than Mom and awkward as a colt, but for a few minutes I felt like Prince Charming, dripping with sophistication, whirling Cinderella around the dance floor. Mom hummed the tune as we moved amidst the crowd and the air carried the sweet-sad strains of a country song, "The Tennessee Waltz."

In the dark, on the ride home, I held in my lap a bottle of soap bubbles received from Santa. It was, I thought, kind of a crummy present. My sister's discarded ball and jacks lay on the car floor. My brother's disheveled jig-saw puzzle lay forgotten in the car seat beneath his sleeping frame. It was the same for everyone, I thought, a Christmas with nothing much. As the old station wagon rolled down the road, telephone poles whizzed past and the countryside glowed from moonlight on scattered patches of snow. The silence in the car accentuated the hiss of tires on pavement. I thought about the Bing Crosby movie with the pretty women in silk dresses dancing beneath diamond chandeliers, the sophisticates dining on champagne and strawberries, the smoothness and shine of their monied lives.

It felt strange, and a little frightening, to realize we were poor. That's what came to me: we were poor people. Like the peons who lined the road as Zorro rode into town. Like the peasants jeering the Hunchback of Notre Dame. We were the rabble, the down-trodden, the backdrop of humanity swathed in rags and hoarsely cheering as Robin Hood emerged from the crowd to rescue Maid Marian. Our family, and most of our friends, we were the ones who get knocked down by the stiff breezes of life, not to mention the storms. We were the ones without fancy clothes or sleek cars or ponies and bicycles for Christmas. And I looked down the road and envisioned a thousand disappointments and deprivations, a thousand offhand slurs, an endless string of troublesome cars and chilly houses and plain meals and cheap entertainment, a lifetime of second best and hand-me-down and sorry, this table is reserved. This shabby Christmas filled me with dismay.

And then I saw out the car window the moonlit snow and streaks of stars. In the front seat my parents switched on the car radio and smiled at Bing Crosby's mellow baritone crooning. My brother began softly snoring and my little sister in her sleep leaned on me. I thought about Craft Hall, the happy, lively people in that crowd. Christmas seemed less disappointing because everyone shared, so perhaps community can dilute disappointment. On second thought, really, it was a pretty good Christmas. The tuna casserole had been tasty, and I got to play Chopsticks on the piano, and my friend Janine taught me to play jacks. There was so much smiling, laughter and dancing. The Christmas party was like the smell of fresh bread still warm from the oven, infusing everything – the tires hiss and the wet streets and the quiet breathing of my family – with some elemental goodness. My mind flip-flopped, and it occurred to me that rich and poor do not much matter, how even the simplest things, soap bubbles or dancing or starlight, make us all rich beyond imagining. And I was for a moment very proud of my mind, to have seen past petty disappointments and absorb the blessing it was to be alive in this one inimitable moment. For that one passing moment I felt that I was the richest boy in the world.

Wishing you community this Christmas,

Gary

Advent

[This a fairly recent letter and more topical than most. News of family events belongs in a Christmas letter as surely as bark on a Christmas tree.]

Dear friends and family,

This December we have been awaiting the birth of a child. Ellen's daughter Meagen, out in Portland, was great with child, and she and her husband Jeremy, being the new generation, made elaborate plans for the birth. They arranged for a gentle water birth attended by an experienced midwife, obstetrician, lactation consultant, wise women (the prospective grandmothers), many friends, and a few uninformed onlookers, like me, in case there was a need to boil water. Ellen and I travelled not East but West, Chicago to Portland, guided not by a star but by satellite, to see the new-born child.

Only the kid did not arrive. An appropriately rotund Madonna, yes. Some lively soccer matches in the womb, yes. But the baby was in no hurry to enter this world. Swimming in mommy was just ducky. So we waited. We took a bright morning walk along Salmon Creek. We got lost exploring neighborhoods in neighboring

Vancouver. We watched cable tv. And we waited.

There is something delicious about waiting. Waiting for Christmas to happen when I was younger had me dreaming of miracles – a colossal stationary star, a fresh snowfall, a pine tree sprouted in the living room, flying reindeer, whipped cream in a can. The anticipation sharpened the sense that something wonderful would happen. Sure, we knew in basic outline what Christmas would bring, the sleigh bells hung on the front door, the wreath in the window, fragrant cookies baking and Christmas carols wafting from the radio. Yet we didn't know. It was almost, but not quite, beyond bearing.

Not quite knowing what would happen – and on Christmas anything could happen – was so tantalizing it made a kid squirm with pleasure. Would Santa bring that cherished toy? Would it snow and be perfect for sledding? Would Aunt Ethel bring that dreadful fruitcake, and would Uncle Frank bring a brace of ducks peppered with buckshot? We couldn't know, yet we sort of knew, and we knew it would be wonderful, or maybe it would be a bust, we couldn't know. So we waited.

That first Christmas, the story goes, some folks were waiting and some were not. I imagine that the shepherds around Bethlehem got their socks knocked off when the angels appeared. The shepherds were just hanging out, not expecting anything special, just watching flocks on a moonlit winter night. And then Pow! Wham! A chorus of angels with trumpets and haloes making a big to-do. Quite a surprise.

But three old men from the East knew something was up. They made a long trip on lumpy camels, following a celestial singularity, because they knew, or thought they knew, something wonderful was about to happen. They camped on sand dunes at night, gathered around a small fire of camel chips, staring into cups of stale tea. Cold crept into their old bones. They hardly spoke.

It may be that the Three Kings of Orient weren't so awfully wise. Their guiding star was in the East, and they were from the East (Orient), so maybe they could have just stayed put. And the gifts they brought! Gold and frankincense and myrrh! They should have brought bright crib toys or pacifiers, or at least extra swaddling clothes. Babies don't need gold or perfume. Babies hate myrrh!

The kings waited and Mary and Joseph waited and Meagen and Jeremy waited and we all waited. That's the way it goes sometimes in life. You thrill with anticipation, you wait and you pray and you wish. You dream of what might be, you dream a million possibilities, and then, and then... something.

Waiting brings a letdown some Christmases. You wait and wish and hope for that special toy, and then blooey, it's a bust. The shirt's too small, the necktie's too loud, the dolly has a bad mechanical eye that stays shut so she has a perpetual wink. It hurts to swallow the mediocrity of reality. But you tell yourself, so what if it disappoints? So what if it disappoints a thousand times? So what? There's always next year, and no one can say what it will bring. You have reason to hope, a right to hope, and that feels great. Hope itself is the gift of Christmas.

Some folks can't stand the waiting. Some folks just got to know, even if they cannot really know. Years ago, I visited Delphi up on Mount Parnassus, where the Oracle held forth. The Oracle was a wise consultant, and she knew the harder she made it to obtain, the more respected was the advice. She made it hard to get there, up a winding mountain road, then climbing three flights of marble stairs, then depositing three talents of silver in the priesthood's coffers, just to ask a single question. After all that travel and labor and expense, the answer had to be good. Some questions were momentous: like shall it be peace or war? shall we store the harvest or feed the poor? shall I marry this girl or her sister? The guide told our group that the most frequently asked question of the Oracle of Delphi was "Will it be a boy or a girl?"

Ellen's daughter and her husband were wise young people. They could wait. Despite the ultrasound, despite hints and prognostications from well-meaning standers-by, they did not worry about the gender of their child. It's a new generation, with new ideas about gender. Will it be a boy, will it be a girl, will it be a female doctor or a male nurse? They didn't care. So what?

Then finally, beautifully, miraculously the waiting paid off. On December 17th Meagen delivered a beautiful 8 lb. 7 oz. baby boy. It was a long labor, an exhausting ordeal of poking and prodding and complicated medical procedures. But then, at the best place on Earth, in just the nick of time, a wet droopy rose petal baby came tumbling into our world.

That first Christmas must have been much the same – minus the drugs and surgery and incubator, perambulator, nurses, doctors, video and cell phone updates. A baby was born. A miracle. No doubt the newborn child looked about at the amazed shepherds, dogged kings, angels, townsfolk, oxen and asses. It looked around with that uncanny baby gaze that simultaneously combines wisdom and innocence, and enveloped by the smell of hay, the warmth of the stable and the tenderness of the people, it went to sleep. Peace on Earth.

The season of Advent teaches us the joy of anticipation. It's the wanting, not the having, that keeps us going. We encounter so many dashed plans, disappointed dreams, needs unmet, requirements unrequited, that we sometimes lose hope. But not forever and not for long. C'mon, admit it, cynics and second guessers all, even if life seems a domino line of disappointments, even if the walls are on fire, we are compelled to shrug off doom. To be hopeless is as groundless as being hopeful, and since we cannot positively know, we might as well positively hope.

For this holiday, I wish merry times, and this year especially, hope.

Gary

Home for Christmas

[A letter from a few years back. It seems now like ages ago. Lately the days race by and this century seems in a terrible hurry.]

Dear friends and family,

This year I decided to skip Christmas. What with the move to the West Coast, the grandparenting, the house purchases in Chicago and Vancouver, two cross-continent car trips, furniture purchases, roof repairs, taking down shades and putting up curtains, etc., etc., I simply felt too pooped to yule. I felt about Christmas the way a turkey feels about Thanksgiving.

Or perhaps, I thought, I'd just fake it. Fake Christmas for these fake times. I'd dabble at holiday doings but not put my heart into it. We would have a Christmas tree of sorts, swift gifting, token lights on the house, store-bought cookies and such – all designed for maximum effect with minimal effort.

For a Christmas tree we would just point folks to the back yard. I mean, this is the Pacific Northwest for cryin' out loud. The whole countryside is nothing but Christmas trees. We got fir and holly in our yard and the neighbors sport spruce and pine. For tree decorations we could just toss a box or two of tinsel in the back yard, and let the squirrels and ravens and brisk Columbia Gorge breeze do the rest. You want a bunch of twinkly lights? Look up, my friend, and behold the stars. Knock yourself out.

On the fireplace mantle, stockings would not be hung. Too much work. We might exchange a kiss beneath the mistletoe, if by some chance a clump of mistletoe finds itself growing in the foyer. For Christmas cards we would just respond to all the e-cards we get with "Peace on Earth – Right Back At Ya." A gift for the one-year-old grandson would be obligatory, of course, but at that age the kid would rather play with the packaging than the brightly colored, non-allergenic whatsis inside. Maybe a nicely wrapped present of nice wrappings. For other folks on the Nice List, I'd let my fingers do the shopping. Gift certificates with a suitably treacly message. As Tiny Tim says, "God bless us, Amazon."

And we could pull it off. A fakey, take-it-easy Christmas. A slough-off, goof-off, good-enough Christmas.

But here's an odd thing: somehow that would not feel right.

It's not as though Christmas is critical. Our family isn't exactly Grade A, top-notch, dyed in the wool Christian. Ellen and I have joined the First Unitarian Church of Portland, and that makes us technically Christian although, in the words of Andrew Greer, "There is really no other word for someone who celebrates Christmas and

Easter, even if only as craft projects." We enjoy the traditions of Christmas, the pretty lights and sprightly shops, the vibrant sweaters and luscious sweets and especially the happy and sublime music. But sometimes it seems increasingly strange. In the face of test tube babies and centrifuged sperm and genetically engineered zygotes, what's the big deal with Immaculate Conception? And considering the political turmoil of Arabia, it seems unlikely that one would find one, much less, three, Wise Men of the East. And considering how supersonic jets roar overhead in perfect silence, the idea of a heavenly host hanging in the clouds, serenading shepherds – don't even get me started.

Still, there's a feeling. Somehow Christmas feels sacred. Maybe the feeling arises from the sheer magnitude of it, the breadth and depth of the multifarious ways humans have woven together sacred stories and candy canes and angels and sleigh bells to make this thing we call Christmas. Christmas is a sacred creation as surely as a great pyramid is a sacred creation, an unfurling of a million ardent wishes, a gallant, impossible, ridiculous and nonetheless palpable stream of hope and undilute joy.

Sacred or not, however, this year Christmas felt skippable. The cause was weariness, yes, but also something subtler, a kind of queerness. Something felt wrong; something was missing. That out-of-kilter feeling had been stealing up on me ever since we moved to the

Portland area. It's a nice place, of course, nice people, beautiful Cascade Mountains and a short drive to the Pacific Ocean. A jolly place to live, but it felt odd for Christmas. The people were different (it rains nearly every day in winter and yet no one carries an umbrella). The language was different (they pronounce 'Wilammette' so that it rhymes with 'goddammit'). The food was different (fiddlehead ferns on quinoa). It all felt a bit alien. Not like home.

That's what was missing: the feeling of home. The affection we feel for Christmas is bound up with the affection we feel for home. It's the same, sappy, ineluctable surge of emotion we get when Dorothy in *The Wizard of Oz* says, "Oh, Auntie Em, there's no place like home." It's the heart of that great sappy holiday movie *It's a Wonderful Life*, that paean to Americana and the old home town. It's why radios in December blare sappy tunes like "There's No Place Like Home for the Holidays" and "I'll Be Home for Christmas (if Only in My Dreams)". Christmas is a reminder of the Eden-like innocence of childhood, the wonderful magic of flying reindeer and steering stars and mystic snow. It is the distillate of all the sweet memories of home. Absent a feeling of home, it just feels wrong.

That's how I felt a month ago, but things began to change. We flew back to Chicago again, partly to check on the condo and partly to see some opera (trust me, *Siegfried* is like Chinese water torture for the ears). We discovered that

Chicago was no longer home. I forgot where the light switches were, and I had to relearn the television remote. Was Dearborn east or west of Clark? What was the name of that restaurant we liked down by Watertower Place? We felt like tourists.

When we got back to the West Coast, I knew where to find the light switches. My sock drawer was organized and my tennis shoes handy in the gym bag. We found a great new Thai place just five minutes from our driveway. Raking up needles and fir cones in the backyard released a pleasant piney smell when I stopped to enjoy the sunset from the back deck. I got to liking even the need to yank open our sticky front door.

Slowly and grudgingly I had a change of heart. Maybe Christmas wasn't so sappy after all. Or maybe I'm getting old and overly sentimental, or maybe I have been that way always but now I see it clearly. Doesn't matter. For me the underlying values remain – hope and happiness, hearth and home. Reflecting on his life and achievements, Walt Disney said, "Sure, I know it's corn. But I like corn."

So maybe I will observe Christmas after all. I'll drag a tree absurdly into the living room. I'll hang lights from the eaves to disguise this suburban ranch as an ice palace. I'll send out Christmas cards because the U.S. Postal Service needs work. I might bake cookies. I might even compose a Christmas letter.

All this to evoke an old feeling in a new place. We are home now. Drop by sometime and take a cup of kindness.

Merry Christmas, happy holidays, go home,

Gary

Christmas Tournament

[Adults often take stock of themselves around New Years. They like to review where they have been the past year and where they stand now – job or business or marriage or some such gauge of accomplishment. Many will resolve to do better in the coming year. For children, taking stock happens more off-handedly, as they puzzle over what they want for Christmas. What should I tell Santa to bring? Do I still want to play with dolls, can I ride a two-wheel bike, am I old enough to carry a pocketknife, do I care more about the gift for my girlfriend than the gift for my mother? Each Christmas serves as a pencil line on the wall marking growth over the last year, the difference between last year's benighted child versus this year's older, taller, possibly wiser model. Sometimes the question "What do I want for Christmas" turns into a question of "What do I want to be like this Christmas."]

Dear family, friends and fans,

It was our freshman year in high school as I recall, when Dan tried out for the basketball team. The process was simple: you show up in the gymnasium and participate in a few weeks of team "practice"; the coach checks out your skills, your stamina, your potential for making a contribution to the team; eventually Coach claps on the shoulder the best players, and he tells the others to hit the showers, better luck next season.

In junior high Dan had been too shy and asthmatic to go out for sports. Besides, he had not been blessed with a Michael Jordan type body. In build he was no string bean, more of a lima bean. But Dan was what, thirteen, and a freshman full of dreams and ready for brave beginnings.

He had grown a few inches and slimmed down some over the summer. The old testosterone had begun to kick in and convert baby fat to leg bone and back muscle. Dan got taller without getting noticeably clumsier, which gave him an edge on most of the other guys. Besides, he had practiced a lot.

All that summer and into the fall Dan haunted a neighborhood basketball court. He probably watched a few professional basketball games on television and he might have read a book on strategy and technique. Mostly he played the game, hour after hour bouncing the ball in his basement, down the sidewalks, through parking lots and school yards. He practiced shooting at the backboard and steel hoop erected at the end of a neighbor's flat asphalt driveway. He found a spot, just at the top of the key, where he could dribble two steps to his right, whirl, and launch a jump shot which would sail up and up in a gentle arc, spinning ever so slightly backwards to reduce the momentum and soften the landing as it fell down, down directly through the hoop and swiftly through the strings of the net with a clean, resolute "snap".

Sometimes Dan played pick-up games with neighborhood kids: twenty-one and around-the-world and banner and horse. He would stand at his "sweet spot" at the top of the key and shout, "Hey Joe, hit me!" or "C'mon, Howie, "feed me!" or "Hey, man, pass the ball, will ya, c'mon, I'm open!" He would take the pass, turn to his right, dribble, dribble, whirl and shoot. Clang, rebound, shoot again. Clang, again. Clangagain.

As often as not, he played alone. Over and over, in the baking noontime sun and the humid dusk, he would practice drifting to his sweet spot. Over and over in that long adolescent summer, from bird calls in the morning to bug dances under street lights, he would repeat the right-handed dribble, the whirl, throw in a minuscule head fake, remember to keep the elbow tucked in and the wrist loose and to release the ball from the fingertips. All summer in the heat, and into the long shadows of fall and the chill of early winter, he kept practicing. Over and over, like some Buddhist monk sunk in the pleasant monotony of a mantra, Dan would practice dribbling between his legs, the no-look pass, the pivot to reach his spot and take his shot, rising against the blue sky of morning and the streetlights of evening, seeking the perfect, ineffable Zen swish.

Friends, you may think you know how to daydream. You may think you daydream with the best of them. But until you have been a lonely starstruck teenager taking practice jump shots, you are a dilettante at daydreaming, a dabbler and a piker. You are in thrall to paltry dreams until you have imagined yourself at the apex of glory, a high school basketball tournament, imagined yourself in the nick of time, the last tick of the last second of the championship game, imagined yourself in the jaws of doom, down by one point, imagined the glare of stadium lights and the crush of the crowd and the din of a thousand voices blended into one hoarse scream as you raise the ball overhead, dip at the knees, jump, unfurl the elbows to launch the ball heavenward in a simple parabolic arc that carries with it everything, all the hope and honor and joy you can ever hope to attain. To miss such a shot brings ignominious agony, but to sink it is Nirvana, Valhalla and Disneyland all brought to Earth. In his dreams, of course, Dan always made the shot.

When he stepped onto the gym floor that first day of tryouts, Dan was probably nervous, feeling a little out of place. In the best tradition of boyhood courtesy and affection I welcomed him to the team: "Hey goofball, hey numb-nuts, hey spastic-man, where'd you get those shoes -- out of a cereal box?"

Dan's clothes, that first day of practice, were not quite right. His shoes were unfortunate, brand new, not Converse All-Stars of pungent graying canvas, and not embellished with crude hand-inked slogans. His t-shirt was plain white -- which was okay in the days before logos -- but it was snowy white, not torn, not stained with sweat or mildew or better yet blood, not ripped up a seam in the heat of battle. His socks shone pure white, brand new, preposterously upright.

Beyond the outfit, something more fundamental was wrong, but it was hard to place. At first I thought it might be the knees, because I had never really noticed Dan's knees before, and there in the light of day they made a pretty ghastly sight. When those knees flashed around the gymnasium, like searchlights, strong men were known to whimper and cover their eyes. Flowers wilted as those knees passed by, and cows dried up and hens stopped laying. Horses bolted from their hitching posts when those knees came to town, and the huge flocks of passenger pigeons which had once filled our skies suddenly wheeled and departed, never to return. Those were some really ugly knees.

The problem wasn't entirely knees, however. It was also eyes. Dan was laughably near-sighted. He wore glasses in class and on the school bus and watching television. He had to put on eyeglasses to see far enough to tie his shoes. But on the basketball floor, he wore none. Perhaps his mother told him he would look dashing without glasses, or perhaps his father suggested that he play without them and avoid the expense of breakage, or perhaps Dan thought he would sprint faster without the excess weight. For some reason, now lost in the sands of time, he played sans lens. The lack of glasses made him look funny, kind of naked, and because he had to squint to bring the basketball rim into focus, he had a perpetual scowl.

So, there was Dan. Short, slow, squinting, scowling, with man-killer knees. Not a promising debut for ninth-grade athletics. My first impression was that his case was hopeless and his chances of making the team miniscule. But then I watched him hustle.

Hustle is not a cardinal virtue (faith, hope, charity, hustle). It has somehow gone out of fashion in our times, even in the simplistic sporting life. It has gone the way of decorum, modesty, conversation and passenger pigeons. But in those innocent times of our youth, hustle was an unquestioned good. It showed passion, enthusiasm, stamina and team spirit. Dan was the first one on the practice floor every day. He helped the managers carry duffel bags of gear out to the gym floor. He stretched and clapped and chattered during warm-up calisthenics. He rebounded for other guys when they shot free-throws. While he might miss easy lay-ups during drills, he hustled and chased down all the loose balls. While he might lag behind during team laps, still he put on a sprint so that he never finished last. He had no height to capture rebounds, but he learned to make crisp passes, and every once in a while, during scrimmage, Dan would drift to the top of the key, get a pass, dribble to his right and loft a long arching jumpshot: *oom mahne padme oom mahne padme oom mahne padme* swish.

The coach must have been impressed with something. After a few, days Denny the Stork stopped coming to practice and John Parski fell down while running backward wind sprints and broke his wrist. Dan hung on. Howie Benning was cut, and so too Sonny Miller and Bill Dortmund and the Schiller twins. Two practices went by and Dan was still hustling. Another two days and all the guys who had been playing basketball together since sixth grade began to think of Dan as part of the team.

Dan must have sprouted confidence about that time, because he grew cocky in class. He raised his hand in social studies – a move hitherto unknown – and he explained to the class the difference between a bill and a law. He had a spring in his step as he sauntered the hall; he scotch-taped a picture of Brigette Bardot inside the metal door of his locker; he cut Latin class to dally in the cafeteria with Cheryl Shank, the prettiest girl in the ninth grade. Perhaps the acme of his new world view was the episode of the dangling sneakers.

Our regular algebra teacher fell sick at the onset of the school year and therefore the administration called in a substitute, a Miss Stanner, a young, thin, smiling stick of a woman with badly crooked teeth. She resembled an opossum wearing a heavy cotton sweater and sensible shoes. She greeted us with warmth and enthusiasm, so we knew at once that she was green, a pushover for homework and hopeless at classroom control.

One morning the class bully Harvey Neeley showed up in class, still sweaty from the gym, bearing a pair of gym shoes which he placed under his student chair. Gradually the odor of the sweat-fouled sneakers permeated the classroom. His shoes reeked to the stars. Fellow students subtly scooted their chairs farther and farther away from Neeley. Noses were crinkled, frowns sprouted and small fits of coughing seized the room. Dan leaned between the row of chairs and stage whispered, "Hey, Neeley, something smells."

Miss Stanner was explaining exponents at the blackboard, so she had her back turned and missed the whisper, but when Neeley stood up suddenly, pushing his chair with a bang into the chair behind him, she whirled and found Neeley advancing on Dan with clenched fists. She shocked us all when she shouted "Stop that!" She marched up to Neeley and spoke sternly in his face, "Young man, come with me." Neeley wilted at her tone and followed her from the room like a whipped beagle following a scolding.

For a moment the classroom was silent. This was clearly becoming a banner day in our educations. Dan rose from his seat and picked up the offending sneakers which were tied together by the laces. Dan carried them to the window, flung up the sash and tossed the foul footwear into space. By some act of providence, the sneakers struck a power line attached to the school building and wrapped themselves around the wire in a series of accelerating arcs like a bolo. Dan shut the window and returned to his seat as the class erupted in hoots and laughter. Howie Benning rose from his chair, walked over to Dan and clapped him on the shoulder, speechless with admiration. Cheryl Shank batted her eyes at Dan and his glasses fogged up.

When Miss Stanner returned to the room, the class quickly quieted down and took up the problem of exponents, but from time to time, boys and girls glanced out the window at the dangling sneakers, lending their perfume to the school yard. Classmates winked at Dan, smiles grew broader, and gradually hilarity from suppressed guffaws and giggles built up like steam pressure. When the bell rang for passing in the hall, the students burst from the classroom flooding the hallways with raucous laughter, leaving Miss Stanner wondering what was so funny about exponents.

Dan was cut from the freshman team the next night. I didn't see it, of course. It was just that Dan and Lou and Popovich didn't show up for practice, not that night or ever again. I didn't think much about it at the time, being absorbed quickly by my own affairs. When I try to imagine what it must have meant to Dan, I keep coming up with a line Bogart delivered in an old movie:

"There's a guy standing in the rain with a comical look on his face because somebody just kicked his guts out."

Dan sort of disappeared for the next several weeks. He was around in body, of course, slouching through the school hallways and snoring in the back row of the auditorium during the school-wide assembly on how to hide under your desk in case of a thermonuclear attack. Dan disappeared like a chameleon, fading into the scuffed hallway paint.

Thanksgiving passed in a blur. Basketball practice heated up and the team spent long hours after school making the gymnasium ring with shouts, whistles and the slap of rubber shoes on a hardwood floor. Christmas came, bringing cold days and television nights. It was pleasant to be off school for two weeks, and to play parcheesi with my family, and eat turkey dinner and open presents with the folks, all the usual stuff. But I missed my friends at school. Tinsel and turkey and toys under the tree were all very fine – but what really mattered was high school and the upcoming basketball tournament.

Just a few days after Christmas and before New Year's, our school was consumed with the annual Christmas Tournament. The event drew a crowd of visitors too, folks from out-of-town and alumni and local sports reporters. The school went all out with banners and posters and a rally to promote the long weekend event. The school band worked up new numbers for the half-time show, the pom-pom squad got spiffy new outfits, the concession stand stocked extra popcorn, and the school superintendent walked around rubbing his hands together, with a big grin in anticipation of the extra revenue. The Christmas Tournament set the stage for high school glory.

On Thursday evening, the eight teams in our conference played the first (quarterfinal) round. As a member of the freshman squad, I did not suit up for varsity games, but all the boys on the freshman team were admitted to the games for free. We sat together about midway up the bleachers. Our coach said to watch closely and learn something. We chomped on popsicles, threw paper airplanes, and mostly we watched the varsity cheerleaders.

None of the four games on Thursday was close. The bigger schools had taller, faster and better coached squads, and, as expected, easily defeated teams from small farming communities outside town. We beat Jerseyville 57-41 and the next round would have us playing the lowest seeded team remaining. Our athletic department wanted to assure the home team a good chance to become champions. All four losing teams went back home for the weekend. So long, losers.

On Friday morning I walked downtown to window shop and work off nervous energy. I did not have any particular thing in mind, just hanging around and soaking up the atmosphere. Streetlights were decked with swirls of greenery.

Banners proclaiming Seasons Greetings shouted from the telephone poles. Shops were hung with holly wreaths and red ribbon. People were out shopping and chatting and just walking around to enjoy the brisk air and holiday music tinkling from speakers on the street lights.

Dan was just leaving the pharmacy shop as I strolled by. His arms were loaded with packages and he showed me the bunion pads and medicines he had picked up "for my Mom". I started to ask where he had been the last couple of weeks, but he was in a hurry and brushed me off. "Sorry, got to run," he said. "See you at the game."

Semi-final tournament games were held late Friday morning. This was partly to be sure that the winning teams would have time to rest before the finals that night and partly to build box office for the evening game. I overslept a little, so I had to rush from the house still munching a piece of Mom's cinnamon toast. As it turned out, I need not have rushed. The game started late and the gymnasium was nearly empty. Referees' whistles echoed in the high empty vault of the auditorium, and the players gym shoes squeaked in the relative silence. Our team won a close game, and it was good basketball, but the victory seemed hollow because only a handful of us watched it. I bade my pals good-bye at the parking lot and walked home puzzled. We had won, we were in the finals, this was the Christmas Tournament for pity's sake! The culmination of weeks and weeks of exhausting practice! A chance to bring fame and honor to our town! Where was everybody?

The day dragged on. Canasta games at the kitchen table bored me; television cartoons with singing elves proved too juvenile. When I complained, Mom put me to work. By late afternoon, I had swept the kitchen, scoured the bathroom, and hauled the trash to the alley, but a dozen more chores remained on Mom's list. I threw on a jacket and slipped down the alley into chill evening air. During the walk to high school, automobile traffic picked up and a few pedestrians passed me in a hurry. I spied the remnants of the tissue-paper float that led the afternoon pep rally. This was more like it. Arriving at the high school parking lot, I spotted scores of cars, and more arriving by the minute. Inside the gymnasium, voices hummed and popcorn aroma filled the hallways. A number of spectators had flung down their winter coats and seated themselves in the bleachers. A hubbub of conversation and chairs scraping and children whining and doors whooshing rose into the great barn we called Memorial Auditorium.

The gymnasium quickly filed with eager townsfolk. Custodians in khaki work pants swept the hardwood floor with long-handled push brooms as the crowd pressed earnestly into the gym. Background chatter rose to a low roar as my pals from the freshman team arrived by twos and threes. We made a noisy cheering bloc as we claimed pretty good seats in the bleachers about ten rows off the floor. We watched the varsity teams rumble out of the tunnels onto the floor for warm-up shooting. Gorgeous in satin jackets they began a weaving lay-up drill. The high school band broke into a rowdy rendition of Sha-Boom-Sha-Boom. The cheerleaders formed a twelve-legged pyramid. The hubbub was rising and people were settling into bleacher seats as I breathed in the adrenaline aura and surveyed the crowd. The night was becoming electric.

On the first row of the gymnasium, right at floor level, sat Dan. I told my buddies l was going to the restroom, but actually I stepped down the bleacher tiers to get near Dan. "Hey," I said to him. "You can't sit there. That's the scorer's table."

Dan beamed at me. "Yeah, I know. I've been keeping statistics for the team. Coach said I could sit at the scorer's table for the finals and help out."

At that moment one of the adults who tended the scoreboard hove into view. He frowned at me. "You can't stand there," he said. "This is the officials' seating area." He waved me aside with the back of his hand. Abashed and stinging from envy, I returned to my seat in the bleachers and watched in amazement as the varsity game started and Dan sat there absorbing everything from the best seat in the house. In a spiral-bound binder Dan jotted down notes. He was keeping track of fouls so he could warn the referees if some player had accumulated five fouls and fouled out.

The game heated up and the home town crowd began to throb with alternate spasms of joy and agony, but I lost interest in it. My gaze was fixed on Dan sitting at the scorer's table, busy scribbling notes, chatting with the men who ran the event. Once a loose ball bounced up on the scorer's table and Dan caught it, and grinning wildly, passed it back to the officials. Watching the game unfold, I felt strange, as though I were walking on the bottom of the ocean amidst waving seaweed and swarming schools of fish. Currents of envy washed over me – what a choice seat Dan had obtained – and then wonder – where did Dad learn to hobnob with adults – and then a pang of vague humiliation – because, while Dan had been making himself useful, I had been caught up in childish stuff – yuletide glitter and bouncy balls and schoolboy glory.

Dan sat at coach's side all season. He tracked each player's shooting percentage, foul shot percentage, rebounds per minute played and other stats. The players followed what he was doing, and the varsity coach appreciated the numbers. It helped pinpoint weaknesses, shore up the defense and supercharge the offense. It helped make us a better team.

Many years have passed since the Christmas Tournament. Dan is grown up now, and he has teenaged children of his own to raise.

His hang-time is nanoseconds, and his fadeaway jumpshot has faded away. He remains a fan.

When I think back on those old high school days, I think that Dan's brief basketball infatuation, and abrupt deflation, and subsequent accommodation were a sort of lesson that we soaked up subconsciously along with exponents and biology and social studies. Not that I ever tried to put it in words back then ... but here goes now:

The lesson to be taken from this sports story is that you should not limit yourself to daydreams about a singular heroic act in one special place at a freeze-frame stupendously magnificent instant of time. You should instead be prepared to accept alternatives, and to so invest yourself in the alternatives that they become precious, momentous and revelatory. Wherever you find yourself is a sweet spot.

Happy holidays. Clangagain.

Gary

Bonfire

[*Most of these Christmas letters could have been written anytime, since one holiday follows another, year after year, in patterns that repeat like choruses of a Christmas carol. This letter could appear toward the front of this book because it depicts my childhood fascination, or toward the middle of the book because it contains an anecdote from my years as a parent. But this letter comes last because it feels more like an ending. Some say the world will end in ice; some say fire.*]

Dear family and friends,

I love a wood fire. As long as I can remember, a real wood fire has brought me comfort and a companionable respite from the cold and dark. Perhaps you, too, have memories of watching a wood fire. Perhaps it was a warming fire at the base of a sledding hill, or a roaring fire at a scout camp, where the counselors gathered the children to hear scary stores of sea monsters and cave creatures and things that whisper in the dark. Perhaps it was a bonfire on the beach, flickering against the soft wash of waves, after the sunset smeared the ocean orange and then rose and then lavender and then black. Perhaps it was a huge fire of discarded two-by-fours at a high school football rally, or when you returned from a hayride to sit by the fire on a crisp October evening, sipping warm cider and watching flames dance among the shadows. Perhaps it was a small campfire at dawn in dark pine woods, wood smoke mingling with the smell of bacon and coffee as mist burned off the lake. Perhaps it was a calm fire at your grandfather's hearth, flickering on cheerful faces, with Christmas candles gauzy in the background.

My own grandfather had no wood fire, despite the fact that he farmed forty acres and had plenty of fallen trees in the woods out back of the corn fields. Grandpa had a coal stove in the center of his small farm house. A wood fire would have been a decoration, a luxury compared to the efficiency of a coal fire. Later he converted the coal stove to an oil furnace. The family was happy to consume the noxious fumes of fuel oil rather than shiver before a meager wood fire. Some folks may pooh-pooh the idea of burning fossil fuels on this warming planet, but they criticize from the comfort of homes with central heating. For much of the world, it's fossil fuel or damn cold.

A big wood fire is such a bonny thing that the boon of it may be ensconced in the language. That immortal hero of the English language, Dr. Samuel Johnson, thought that the term "bonfire" came from the French "bon" meaning "good," but modern scholars claim that the word comes from Late Middle English, a combination of "bone" plus "fire", denoting a large open-air fire in which bones were burnt as part of pagan sacrifices. Sorry Dr. Johnson, the moderns are probably right. Outdoor fires play a role in folk traditions in all parts of the world and have been central to gatherings and celebrations since prehistory. Think of Walpurgis night in Germany or the festival of Lohri in India or even Burning Man in Nevada. In lower Louisiana on Christmas Eve, folks build bonfires along the Mississippi River levees to light the way for Papa Noël as he glides down the river in a pirogue pulled by eight alligators. Bonfires and 'gators, you got to love Louisiana.

What is it about a fire anyway? Warmth certainly. After a morning of tromping through snow drifts, snowball fights, sledding, skating and snow angels and so becoming blue with cold, approaching a fireplace is sheer delight. To sit beside a cheery fire, growing warm and perhaps drowsy and listening to old stories while the fire hisses and crackles, is to soak up quiet, snuggly joy. The hearth since ancient times has been the very heart of home.

Yet it's more than warmth. It delights all the senses. The smell of a wood fire, like the smell of burning leaves, releases deep memories of harvest time, a time to relax and lie fallow, a time for comfort, safety and the excited blood that comes from a gathering of the tribe. Fire brings illumination of course. Abe Lincoln, they say, grew up a poor farmer's boy who depended for his education on flickering firelight. He read his Bible by firelight and worked his sums with the soot of scorched twigs. In Lincoln's time and for countless preceding generations, the fire was for cooking too, and the charm of firelight must have amplified the aroma of baking cornbread and squirrel stew.

Yet it's something more. If you are like me, you have been mesmerized by firelight. You have stared into dancing flames and watched embers glow and sparks fly up into the starry sky, and the fire brought you tireless delight, a shifting mystery, a trancelike fascination. A bonfire is sublime. The pleasure we feel watching fire's endless variations, the dance of flames, the pulsing of coals, is the same thing we feel watching a snowfall, or a waterfall, or the stars in the night sky. This perception was described by the philosopher Immanuel Kant, in his early essay "On the Beautiful and Sublime". Kant wrote that we have two distinct, but often confounded, aesthetic responses. We respond to the "beautiful" -- which since Aristotle has been identified as "the perception of order within multiplicity," like seeing an exuberance of petals on a flower neatly arrayed. And we get a subtly different feeling when we perceive multiplicity without order, the "sublime," like beholding myriads of stars in the night sky, an enormity which both overwhelms and lifts the mind. A lively bonfire is like a gift from the gods, an experience of the sublime on a human scale.

One fire that still glows in my memory burned on the banks of the Fox River where my young family gathered to ice skate on Christmas

Eve many years ago. My good neighbor Bob helped me clear a space on the dappled blue ice of a frozen pond. We chopped a hole at the edge of the ice to confirm that it was at least four inches thick and safe for skating. We mamboed to the roar of snow-blowers as we cleared a patch on a wind-sheltered lagoon and so created a skating rink amid the snowy woods. My wife and I, our kids, Bob and his wife and child and a gradually thickening neighborhood crowd drifted onto the pond just as the sun was setting. For hours we glided over the nubby ice, playing Crack-the-Whip and a game the kids invented called Pom-Pom-Pullaway. Skates cutting dark ice made a crisp keening, the air was laced with pine scent, and the moon rose over the lagoon surface shining like a black mirror. We zoomed with abandon over the center of the pond, but hop-stepped with care along the edges where reeds and twigs protruded from the thin ice. We built a fire from twigs and fallen branches, and then we added logs from the driftwood that clogged the river shore. Later that evening we would change into festive clothes and traipse the neighborhood, singing Christmas carols to friends, strangers, one and all. But for two or three sweet hours we communed before a bonfire, sometimes breathless and sometimes chatty, huddling under blankets between sorties on the ice. A skater would thrust her ankles toward the flames, still encased in skates so tightly laced that they cut off the circulation, and gradually the toes unfroze so that they stung when warmth returned. Hot chocolate spread through the rib cage like a lava flow, and a person grew quiet, brimming with content. You could watch the flames forever.

I think I want to end up fire. We speak of purifying fire, a bonfire of vanity, a burning of effigies to rid us of demons and make a clean start. In a long life, when I think of all the snubs and stubs of living, all those cold shoulders and closed doors, all that swallowing pride and eating crow, the disappointments that sink to weary despair, it seems that living means accumulating a heap of dross. This year on my birthday, I felt the weight of so many years, such a lot of dross. In that mood I instructed my good wife (and pal and counselor and co-conspirator and executrix) when I die to have me cremated. I want my remains to go in a great, good fire – not because I want to feign humility, not because I want to save the Earth from my pollutant remains, not because I'm claustrophobic or afraid of worms, not to avoid the waste space from the petty memorial of a grave – but because I want my remains to be purified in fire. I want the greater part of me, the water content, to swell, boil and burst through cell walls and then rise as water vapor, a mist, so that I might come back as a rainbow. I want the dross part of me turned into weightless ash, so that I might rise as dust particles and so instigate a snowfall. I want for memorial only some memories lingering in the minds of family and friends, just an ember glowing and receding with a hiss.

Merry Chrisssmasssss

Made in the USA
Columbia, SC
24 October 2020